easy meals cooked in just
one pot

easy meals cooked in just
one pot

Make life simple with over 70 delicious one-pot, slow-cooked recipes

Consultant Editor Jenni Fleetwood

southwater

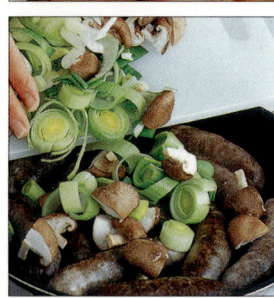

This edition is published by Southwater

Southwater is an imprint of Anness Publishing Ltd
Hermes House, 88–89 Blackfriars Road, London SE1 8HA
tel. 020 7401 2077; fax 020 7633 9499
www.southwaterbooks.com; info@anness.com

© Anness Publishing Ltd 2005

UK agent: The Manning Partnership Ltd
6 The Old Dairy, Melcombe Road, Bath BA2 3LR
tel. 01225 478444; fax 01225 478440; sales@manning-partnership.co.uk

UK distributor: Grantham Book Services Ltd
Isaac Newton Way, Alma Park Industrial Estate, Grantham, Lincs NG31 9SD
tel. 01476 541080; fax 01476 541061; orders@gbs.tbs-ltd.co.uk

North American agent/distributor: National Book Network
4501 Forbes Boulevard, Suite 200, Lanham, MD 20706
tel. 301 459 3366; fax 301 429 5746; www.nbnbooks.com

Australian agent/distributor: Pan Macmillan Australia
Level 18, St Martins Tower, 31 Market St, Sydney, NSW 2000
tel. 1300 135 113; fax 1300 135 103; customer.service@macmillan.com.au

New Zealand agent/distributor: David Bateman Ltd
30 Tarndale Grove, Off Bush Road, Albany, Auckland
tel. (09) 415 7664; fax (09) 415 8892

All rights reserved. No part of this publication may be reproduced, stored in a retrieval system, or transmitted in any way or by any means, electronic, mechanical, photocopying, recording or otherwise, without the prior written permission of the copyright holder.

A CIP catalogue record for this book is available from the British Library.

Publisher: Joanna Lorenz
Editorial Director: Helen Sudell
Editors: Jennifer Schofield and Elizabeth Woodland
Editorial Reader: Richard McGinlay
Designer: Nigel Partridge
Cover Designer: Whitelight Design
Photography: James Duncan, Ian Garlick, Michelle Garrett, Amanda Heywood, David Jordan, Dave King, William Lingwood, Patrick McLeavey, Thomas Odulate, Craig Robertson, Sam Stowell
Recipes: Alex Barker, Michelle Berriedale-Johnson, Kit Chan, Jacqueline Clarke, Matthew Drennan, Sarah Edmonds, Joanna Farrow, Brian Glover, Nicola Graimes, Christine Ingram, Lucy Knox, Lesley Mackley, Sally Mansfield, Sallie Morris, Jennie Shapter, Anne Sheasby, Steven Wheeler, Kate Whiteman, Jeni Wright
Production Controller: Wendy Lawson

Previously published as part of a larger volume, *One Pot: Slow-cooked Recipes without the Fuss*

1 3 5 7 9 10 8 6 4 2

NOTES
Bracketed terms are for American readers.

For all recipes, quantities are given in both metric and imperial measures and, where appropriate, measures are also given in standard cups and spoons. Follow one set, but not a mixture because they are not interchangeable.

Standard spoon and cup measures are level. 1 tsp = 5ml,
1 tbsp = 15ml, 1 cup = 250ml/8fl oz

Australian standard tablespoons are 20ml. Australian readers should use 3 tsp in place of 1 tbsp for measuring small quantities of gelatine, cornflour, salt etc.

Medium (US large) eggs are used unless otherwise stated.

CONTENTS

Introduction 6

One-pot Equipment 8

One-pot Cooking Techniques 10

Soups 12

Meat and Game 26

Chicken and Poultry 40

Fish and Shellfish 54

Vegetarian and Pasta 68

Side Dishes 82

Index 96

Introduction

What do spicy stir-fries, nourishing soups, delectable stews, robust roasts, and creamy risottos have in common? They are all one-pot dishes, easy to prepare, a pleasure to serve and the perfect choice for family and friends.

Elaborate dinner parties are a rarity these days. On the menu instead are simple dishes prepared with the minimum of fuss but with maximum flavour. Even celebrity chefs have turned their backs on fiddly food, preferring instead to take a second look at old favourites like Irish Stew, Fillet of Beef Stroganoff and Ratatouille. Coq au Vin has also made a come-back, and it is gaining new converts among a generation that has never tasted that delicious combination of chicken, red wine, bacon and shallots.

Cooking in a single pot is wonderfully liberating. All that is needed is a bit of leisurely preparation, and then you can relax, secure in the knowledge that there will be no last-minute sauces to make or tricky toppings to produce. Serving a selection of side dishes is largely unnecessary, especially when the recipe includes vegetables, so you have the perfect excuse for sparing yourself the anxiety that comes with trying to have the main meal and side dishes ready all at the same time.

Bread is the ideal partner for one-pot dishes. Not only do golden-crusted loaves fit the rustic, relaxed atmosphere that is part of the whole experience, but guests always enjoy tearing off chunks and using them to mop up every bit of the delicious sauce.

Above: Paella, a classic one-pot seafood and rice dish from Spain, is traditionally cooked in a shallow, two-handled pan.

Left: A whole chicken cooked with forty cloves of garlic makes the perfect pot-roast, and like other one-pot dishes, needs little attention once it is in the oven.

Below: Using a clay pot to cook one-pot recipes, such as this spinach and sweet potato dish, can be good for you. The clay pot ensures that the vitamins and minerals of the ingredients are retained.

If you have the time and the inclination you could make your own bread, matching the flavour of the central dish. For example, herb bread would be very welcome with Venison Sausages with Red Wine Gravy, while for something with a Mediterranean flavour, ciabatta or a bread made with sun-dried tomatoes would be ideal.

For one-pot dishes that already include starch, in the form of rice, potatoes or pasta, a simple salad might be a better choice as an accompaniment than bread. Try to include crisp ingredients, like fennel, celery or peppers, to provide a contrast in texture to the tenderness of the long-cooked meat or fish, and keep the dressing simple, so it does not vie with the flavours in the casserole or stew.

One-pot dishes also tend to be fairly good-natured, and will seldom spoil if not eaten the moment they are ready. Some dishes, like curries and casseroles, will improve if made the day before, so that all the flavours can bed down together and blend. Stir-fries, pasta and rice dishes need last-minute cooking, but if the preparation is done in advance, the effort is minimal.

One-pot cooking is perfect for everyone, from students with a single hot plate to families feeding in relays. Dishes can be cooked in the oven, on top of the stove or in a free-standing appliance like a microwave oven.

There is also very little washing up, and if there are any leftovers, you may well be able to transform them into tasty pie fillings, simply by sandwiching them inside ready-rolled puff pastry or filo.

One-pot cooking is also extremely healthy, especially if you are using a clay pot. The pots ensure that most of the vitamins and minerals found in the ingredients are retained. This ancient form of cooking seals in the food's natural juices by enclosing it in a porous clay container that has been soaked in water. As the container heats up, the water turns to steam, keeping the contents moist and tender. The only other liquid used in clay-pot cooking is that which comes from the food itself, so that its full flavour can be appreciated.

Left: *This spicy and aromatic Moroccan fish tagine is just one delicious dish that proves that fish is not only a wonderfully versatile and nutritious ingredient, but it should not be excluded from one-pot cooking.*

Below: *One-pot cooking doesn't have to take hours. Stir-fries are quick and easy to cook and are also wonderfully tasty.*

ONE-POT EQUIPMENT

If you are going to do a lot of cooking in just one pot, make it a good one. There's no point in planning a pot-roast for the whole family, only to find you haven't got a big enough pan, or that the one you have has a wobbly base. It is equally irritating to discover that your only decent casserole has a crack in it, or can only be used in the oven and not on top of the stove. Choose your cookware with care; it is worth investing in good quality equipment that will last.

Right:
Stainless-steel pans with a heavy base are a good choice for one-pot cooking.

Above: Frying pans with metal handles can be used under the grill (broiler) and in the oven.

For one-pot cooking, you need a large pan with a heavy base, which will conduct the heat evenly and help to prevent the food from scorching should you inadvertently allow the amount of liquid to get too low. A good quality stainless-steel pan would be an excellent choice, but it is important to choose one with an aluminium or copper base, since stainless steel does not conduct heat well. For long, slow cooking, cast-iron pans coated in vitreous enamel are ideal, as they can also be used in the oven. When buying a frying pan, choose one with a heavy base. When cooking a frittata or a dessert such as tarte Tatin, it is essential to use a frying pan with a handle that can withstand the heat of the grill (broiler) or oven; a point worth considering when you are buying a new frying pan.

Woks

One of the most useful items in the kitchen, the wok need not be reserved solely for stir-frying. It is the ideal pan for quick-cooked creamy dishes such as beef Stroganoff. The wok can also be used for making a risotto. Woks that

Pots and Pans

When you are buying cooking equipment, it is very tempting to opt for a set of shiny pans, rather than individual items that might suit your purposes — and your personal circumstances — better.

Below left: A large pot with metal handles can be used on top of the stove and in the oven.

Left:
Woks have either one or two handles.

One-pot Equipment 9

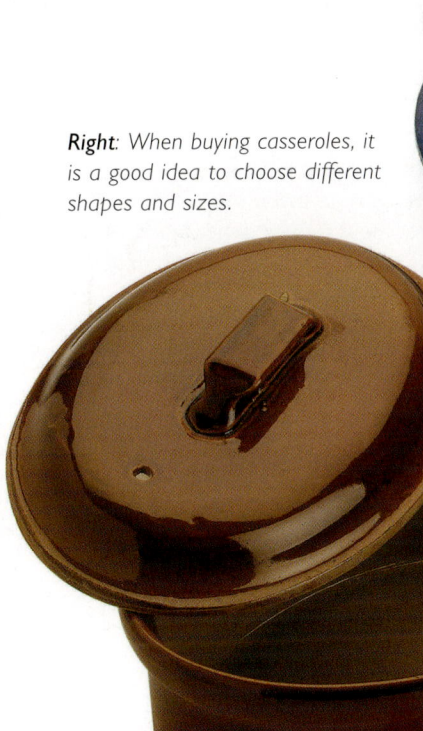

Right: When buying casseroles, it is a good idea to choose different shapes and sizes.

Casseroles

For one-pot cooking, choose a casserole that is big enough to serve six, even if you usually cook for four.

This will give you plenty of room for stirring the contents without risking splashes and scalds. The ideal pot will be one that can be used on top of the stove as well as inside it, so that if you do need to do any pre-cooking, or if cooking juices need to be reduced by boiling, you will not need a second container. If you buy several casseroles, vary the shapes as well as the sizes. For cooking a whole chicken, for instance, an oval is more useful than a round dish. Look at the handles, too. It is important that they are easy to grasp, and that they do not become so hot that they are liable to burn you, even when you are using an oven glove. Appearance will obviously be a consideration, since you will be serving straight from the casserole, but consider practical aspects too.

have a flat base can be used on all types of cooker. They can have either one or two handles. Those with two handles are good for deep-frying and general cooking, while the wok with one handle is designed especially for stir-frying. The single handle makes the wok easy to pick up so that the ingredients can be stirred and tossed in the wok at the same time.

FREE-STANDING ELECTRIC COOKING POTS

It isn't vital to have a stove in order to cook a one-pot meal. Electric frying pans; slow-cookers (and combinations of the two); multi-purpose appliances, in which you can shallow fry, deep-fry or even cook a casserole, all have the advantage that they have easy temperature control, use very little electricity and are easy to clean.

Baking Dishes

There are plenty of one-pot recipes that benefit from being cooked in large, shallow dishes, from oven-roasted vegetables to layered potato bakes. Buy several different shapes, bearing in mind the size of your oven. Having two rectangular dishes that will fit side by side can be a real boon if you want to cook one meal for serving immediately and another for the freezer.

Ramekins

You will also find it useful to have six or eight ovenproof ramekin dishes, for baking single portions, such as individual soufflés and oven-baked desserts.

Below: Choose two ovenproof baking dishes that will fit next to each other in your oven.

FLAMEPROOF CASSEROLES

The most versatile casseroles are also flameproof and so can be used on top of the stove and under the grill (broiler) as well as in the oven.

ONE-POT COOKING TECHNIQUES

Cooking a dish in a single pot doesn't demand any particular expertise, but mastering a few simple techniques will make for greater efficiency, especially when preparing the ingredients. Many one-pot dishes need very little attention while they are actually cooking, but it is important to follow the instructions in individual recipes as regards stirring.

Stewing, Braising and Casseroling Meat
These are long, slow and moist methods of cooking either in the oven or on top of the stove. The meat is browned first to seal in the natural juices and improve the flavour and colour of the finished dish, then it is simmered slowly at a low temperature in liquid – wine, water, beer or stock.

1 Trim off any excess fat from the meat. For stewing and casseroling, cut the meat into 2.5cm/1in cubes. For braising use thickly cut steaks or cut the meat into thick slices.

2 Toss the meat a few pieces at a time in seasoned flour, then shake off any excess. The flour coating browns to give the casserole a good flavour and also thickens the liquid.

3 Heat 30ml/2 tbsp sunflower oil in a flameproof casserole. Add the meat in batches and cook over a high heat. When the meat is well browned on all sides, use a draining spoon to remove the meat before adding the next batch.

4 Add the sliced or chopped onions and other vegetables to the remaining fat and juices in the casserole and cook, stirring occasionally, for about 5 minutes.

5 Return the meat to the casserole, add herbs and pour in the cooking liquid. Stir to loosen the cooking residue from the base of the pan and then heat until simmering. Simmer gently on the hob or in the oven until the meat is tender. The casserole may be covered for the entire cooking time or uncovered towards the end to allow excess liquid to evaporate.

> ### CUTS FOR STEWS, BRAISES AND CASSEROLES
> These slow-cooked dishes are ideal for tough, inexpensive cuts of meat, such as cubes of stewing steak or slices of braising steak, less tender cuts of lamb such as shoulder, and diced or thickly sliced pork. Lamb leg steaks, although fairly tender, are also a good choice for braising.

Pot-roasting Meat
This long, slow method of cooking is ideal for slightly tough joints of meat such as topside of beef, lamb shoulder and shanks, and knuckle of pork.

1 Heat a little sunflower oil in a large flameproof casserole until very hot. Add the meat and cook over a high heat, turning frequently, until browned on all sides. Remove the meat from the pan.

2 Add the onions, leeks and any root vegetables to the pan, then cook, stirring, for a few minutes. Replace the meat on top of the vegetables and pour in a little liquid, such as stock, wine or beer. Cover and cook gently in the oven until the meat is tender.

One-pot Cooking Techniques

Casseroling Chicken

Moist cooking methods not only bring out the flavour of poultry but also offer the opportunity for allowing herbs and spices and aromatics to infuse the light meat thoroughly. Whole birds and joints can be casseroled.

1 Brown the poutry pieces or bird all over first. Remove from the pan before softening chopped onion, carrot, celery and other flavouring ingredients in the fat remaining in the pan.

2 Replace the poultry before adding the chosen liquid – stock, wine or canned tomatoes. Season the casserole well, then bring it just to simmering point. Cover it closely and allow it to simmer very gently on top of the stove, or cook in the oven at 180°C/350°F/Gas 4.

> **COOKING TIMES FOR CASSEROLING CHICKEN**
> • For a whole bird allow 20 minutes per 450g/1lb, plus 20 minutes.
> • Large portions 45–60 minutes.
> • Boneless breasts about 30 minutes.
> • Chunks or diced poultry 20–40 minutes, depending on their size.

Pan-frying Meat

This is the traditional cooking method for steaks such as sirloin and fillet, and it is also good for veal escalopes (US scallops) and veal chops, lamb chops, cutlets and noisettes, and pork chops, steaks and escalopes.

1 Cook steaks and chops in the minimum of fat, then add flavoured butter when serving, if you like. Dab a little sunflower oil on kitchen paper and use to grease the pan lightly. Heat the pan until it is very hot (almost smoking). Add the steak or chops and cook for 2–4 minutes on each side.

2 Pan-fry other lean cuts of meat in a mixture of butter and oil. Butter burns easily, so heat the oil in the pan first and add the butter just before the meat to avoid this. Make sure that the butter and oil are sizzling before adding the meat. Cook on both sides until browned. Beef and thin cuts of meat such as escalopes will be ready to serve. For some thicker cuts and meat such as pork that needs to be well-cooked, reduce the heat to low once the meat is browned and cook for 10–15 minutes, or until cooked through. Test by piercing the centre of the meat with the point of a sharp knife.

Pan-frying Poultry

This quick cooking method is ideal for chicken breast fillets and portions. Once the meat is cooked, the cooking juices can be made into a tasty sauce, simply stir in a little cream, add some chopped herbs and season to taste.

When frying poultry, remember that it must be cooked through. Escalopes and boneless breasts cook quickly, so are ideal for pan-frying over a high heat, but uneven thicker portions require careful cooking. With larger pieces, reduce the heat to low once the chicken is browned and cook it slowly for up to 30 minutes to ensure that the centre is cooked.

Stir-frying

This is a fast method of cooking tender meat. The meat should be cut into thin slices across the grain, and then cut into fine, long strips. Use a wok or a heavy frying pan.

Heat a little oil in a wok or frying pan until it is smoking hot. Add the meat in batches and stir-fry over a high heat. Remove the cooked meat before adding a fresh batch. When all the meat is cooked, add the other ingredients and stir-fry over a slightly lower heat.

SOUPS

There's something supremely comforting about hot soup, and when you prepare it yourself, the aroma ensures that the pleasure starts long before you lift the ladle. Nourishing, easy to digest, quick to cook and convenient, soup provides the perfect meal-in-a-bowl at lunchtime or a warming after-school snack, and when served as a first course, it gives guests a real sense of welcome. Broccoli, Anchovy and Pasta Soup, Mediterranean Sausage and Pesto Soup, Moroccan Spiced Lamb Soup, and Clam, Mushroom and Potato Chowder are just some of the treats in store.

  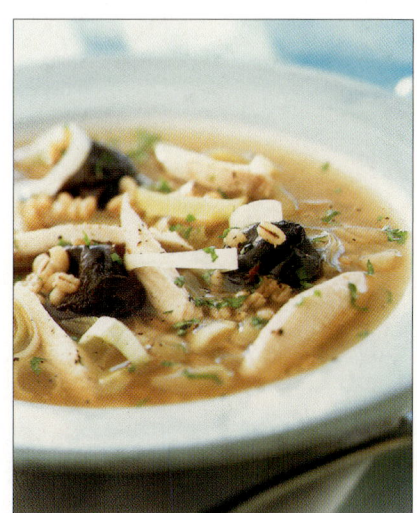

LENTIL and PASTA SOUP

This rustic vegetarian soup makes a warming winter meal and goes especially well with Granary or crusty Italian bread.

SERVES 4–6

175g/6oz/¾ cup brown lentils
3 garlic cloves, unpeeled
1 litre/1¾ pints/4 cups water
45ml/3 tbsp olive oil
25g/1oz/2 tbsp butter
1 onion, finely chopped
2 celery sticks, finely chopped
30ml/2 tbsp sun-dried tomato paste
1.75 litres/3 pints/7½ cups vegetable stock
a few fresh marjoram leaves
a few fresh basil leaves
leaves from 1 fresh thyme sprig
50g/2oz/½ cup dried small pasta shapes, such as macaroni or tubetti
salt and ground black pepper
tiny fresh herb leaves, to garnish

1 Put the lentils in a large pan. Smash one of the garlic cloves using the blade of a large knife (there's no need to peel it first), then add it to the lentils. Pour in the water and bring to the boil. Simmer for about 20 minutes, or until the lentils are tender. Tip the lentils into a sieve, remove the garlic and set it aside. Rinse the lentils under the cold tap and leave to drain.

2 Heat 30ml/2 tbsp of the oil with half the butter in the pan. Add the onion and celery and cook gently for 5 minutes.

3 Crush the remaining garlic, then peel and mash the reserved garlic. Add to the pan with the remaining oil, the tomato purée and the lentils. Stir, then add the stock, herbs and salt and pepper. Bring to the boil, stirring. Simmer for 30 minutes, stirring occasionally.

4 Add the pasta and bring the soup back to the boil, stirring. Reduce the heat and simmer until the pasta is just tender. Add the remaining butter to the pan and stir until melted. Taste the soup for seasoning, then serve hot in warmed bowls, sprinkled with herb leaves.

ITALIAN FARMHOUSE SOUP

Root vegetables form the base of this chunky, minestrone-style main meal soup. You can vary the vegetables according to what you have to hand.

SERVES 4

30ml/2 tbsp olive oil
1 onion, roughly chopped
3 carrots, cut into large chunks
175–200g/6–7oz turnips, cut into large chunks
about 175g/6oz swede (rutabaga), cut into large chunks
400g/14oz can chopped Italian tomatoes
15ml/1 tbsp tomato purée (paste)
5ml/1 tsp dried mixed herbs
5ml/1 tsp dried oregano
50g/2oz dried (bell) peppers, washed and thinly sliced (optional)
1.5 litres/2½ pints/6¼ cups vegetable stock or water
50g/2oz/½ cup dried small macaroni or conchiglie
400g/14oz can red kidney beans, rinsed and drained
30ml/2 tbsp chopped fresh flat leaf parsley
salt and ground black pepper
freshly grated Parmesan cheese, to serve

1 Heat the olive oil in a large pan, add the onion and cook over a low heat for about 5 minutes until softened. Add the carrot, turnip and swede chunks, canned chopped tomatoes, tomato purée, dried mixed herbs, dried oregano and dried peppers, if using. Stir in salt and pepper to taste.

2 Pour in the vegetable stock or water and bring to the boil. Stir well, cover the pan, then lower the heat and simmer for 30 minutes, stirring occasionally.

3 Add the pasta to the pan and bring quickly to the boil, stirring. Lower the heat and simmer, uncovered, for about 5 minutes until the pasta is only just tender, or according to the instructions on the packet. Stir frequently.

4 Stir in the kidney beans. Heat through for 2–3 minutes, then remove the pan from the heat and stir in the parsley. Taste the soup for seasoning. Serve hot in warmed soup bowls, with grated Parmesan cheese handed separately.

BROCCOLI, ANCHOVY and PASTA SOUP

This wonderfully chunky and flavourful soup is from Puglia in the south of Italy, where anchovies and broccoli are often used together.

SERVES 4

30ml/2 tbsp olive oil
1 garlic clove, finely chopped
¼–⅓ fresh red chilli, seeded and finely chopped
2 drained canned anchovies
1 small onion, finely chopped
200ml/7fl oz/scant 1 cup passata (bottled strained tomatoes)
45ml/3 tbsp dry white wine
1.2 litres/2 pints/5 cups vegetable or light chicken stock
300g/11oz broccoli florets
200g/7oz/1¾ cups dried orecchiette pasta or other medium-size pasta shapes
salt and ground black pepper
freshly grated Pecorino cheese, to serve

1 Heat the oil in a large pan. Add the garlic, chilli, anchovies and onion and cook over a low heat, stirring constantly, for 5–6 minutes.

2 Add the passata and wine, with salt and pepper to taste. Bring to the boil, cover, then cook over a low heat, stirring occasionally, for 12–15 minutes.

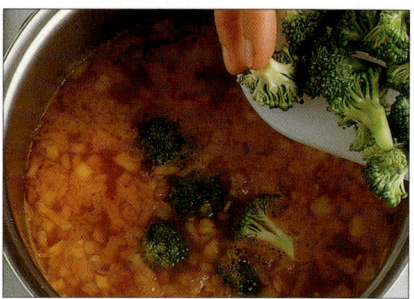

3 Pour in the stock. Bring to the boil, then add the broccoli and simmer for about 5 minutes. Add the pasta and bring back to the boil, stirring. Simmer, stirring frequently for 7–8 minutes until the pasta is just tender, or according to the packet instructions. Taste for seasoning. Serve hot, in warmed bowls. Hand around grated Pecorino separately.

PASTA SQUARES and PEAS in BROTH

This thick, filling Italian soup, flavoured with pancetta or bacon and prosciutto, is traditionally made with home-made pasta and fresh peas. In this modern, more convenient version, ready-made fresh lasagne sheets are used with frozen peas, to save time.

SERVES 4–6

25g/1oz/2 tbsp butter
50g/2oz pancetta or rindless smoked streaky (fatty) bacon, roughly chopped
1 small onion, finely chopped
1 celery stick, finely chopped
400g/14oz/3½ cups frozen peas
5ml/1 tsp tomato purée (paste)
5–10ml/1–2 tsp finely chopped fresh flat leaf parsley
1 litre/1¾ pints/4 cups chicken stock
300g/11oz fresh lasagne sheets
about 50g/2oz prosciutto, cut into cubes
salt and ground black pepper
freshly grated Parmesan cheese, to serve

1 Melt the butter in a large pan and add the pancetta or rindless smoked streaky bacon, with the chopped onion and chopped celery. Cook together over a low heat, stirring constantly, for 5 minutes.

2 Add the frozen peas to the pan and cook, stirring, for 3–4 minutes. Stir in the tomato purée and finely chopped parsley, then add the chicken stock, with salt and pepper to taste. Bring to the boil. Cover, lower the heat and simmer the soup for 10 minutes.

3 Meanwhile, using a large, sharp knife and a ruler, cut the lasagne sheets into 2cm/¾in squares.

4 Taste the soup for seasoning. Drop the pasta into the pan, then stir and bring to the boil. Simmer for 2 minutes, or until the pasta is just tender, then stir in the prosciutto. Serve hot with grated Parmesan handed around separately.

COOK'S TIP
Take care when seasoning the soup with salt, because of the saltiness of the pancetta and the prosciutto.

MEDITERRANEAN SAUSAGE and PESTO SOUP

This hearty soup makes a satisfying one-pot meal that brings the summery flavour of basil to midwinter meals. Thick slices of warm crusty bread make the perfect accompaniment.

SERVES 4

oil, for deep-frying
450g/1lb smoked pork sausages
a handful of fresh basil leaves
15ml/1 tbsp olive oil
1 red onion, chopped
225g/8oz/1 cup red lentils
400g/14oz can chopped tomatoes
  with herbs
1 litre/1¾ pints/4 cups chicken stock
  or water
salt and ground black pepper
60ml/4 tbsp pesto, to serve

COOK'S TIP
The flavour of smoked sausages is very good in this soup, but you could use ordinary fresh sausages if you like. Choose coarse-textured sausages, such as Toulouse.

1 Heat the oil for deep-frying to 190°C/375°F or until a cube of day-old bread browns in about 60 seconds. Slice one of the sausages diagonally and deep-fry for 2–3 minutes, or until brown and crisp. Add the basil leaves and fry for a few seconds until crisp. Lift out the sausage slices and basil leaves using a slotted spoon and drain them on kitchen paper. Strain the oil into a bowl.

2 Heat the olive oil in the pan, add the chopped red onion and cook until softened. Coarsely chop the remaining sausages and add them to the pan. Cook for about 5 minutes, stirring, or until the sausages are cooked.

3 Stir in the lentils, tomatoes and stock or water and bring to the boil. Reduce the heat, cover and simmer for about 20 minutes. Cool the soup slightly before puréeing it in a blender. Return the soup to the rinsed-out pan.

4 Reheat the soup, add seasoning to taste, then ladle into warmed individual soup bowls. Sprinkle the soup with the deep-fried sausage slices and basil and swirl a little pesto through each portion just before serving. Serve with plenty of warm crusty bread.

MOROCCAN SPICED LAMB SOUP

Classic north African spices – ginger, turmeric and cinnamon – are combined with chickpeas and lamb to make this hearty, warming soup.

SERVES 6

75g/3oz/½ cup chickpeas, soaked overnight
15g/½oz/1 tbsp butter
225g/8oz lamb, cut into cubes
1 onion, chopped
450g/1lb tomatoes, peeled and chopped
a few celery leaves, chopped
30ml/2 tbsp chopped fresh parsley
15ml/1 tbsp chopped fresh coriander (cilantro)
2.5ml/½ tsp ground ginger
2.5ml/½ tsp ground turmeric
5ml/1 tsp ground cinnamon
1.75 litres/3 pints/7½ cups water
75g/3oz/scant ½ cup green lentils
75g/3oz vermicelli or soup pasta
2 egg yolks
juice of ½–1 lemon
salt and ground black pepper
fresh coriander (cilantro), to garnish
lemon wedges, to serve

1 Drain the chickpeas, rinse under cold water and set aside. Melt the butter in a large flameproof casserole or pan and fry the lamb and onion for 2–3 minutes, stirring, until the lamb is just browned.

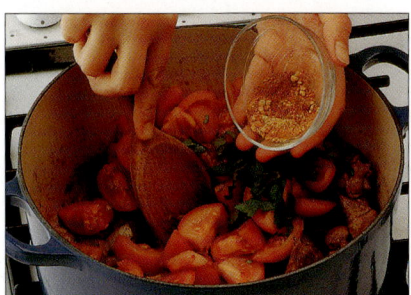

2 Add the chopped tomatoes, celery leaves, herbs and spices and season well with ground black pepper. Cook for about 1 minute, then stir in the water and add the green lentils and the soaked, drained and rinsed chickpeas.

3 Slowly bring to the boil and skim the surface to remove the froth. Boil rapidly for 10 minutes, then reduce the heat and simmer very gently for 2 hours, or until the chickpeas are very tender.

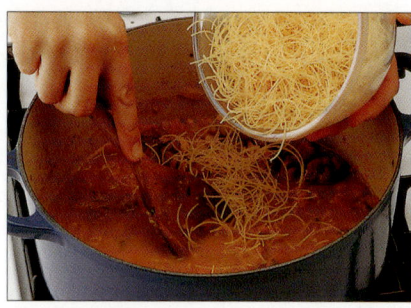

4 Season with salt and pepper, then add the vermicelli or soup pasta to the pan and cook for 5–6 minutes until it is just tender. If the soup is very thick at this stage, add a little more water.

5 Beat the egg yolks with the lemon juice and stir into the simmering soup. Immediately remove the soup from the heat and stir until thickened. Pour into warmed serving bowls and garnish with plenty of fresh coriander. Serve the soup with lemon wedges.

COOK'S TIP

If you have forgotten to soak the chickpeas overnight, place them in a pan with about four times their volume of cold water. Bring very slowly to the boil, then cover the pan, remove it from the heat and leave to stand for 45 minutes before using as described in the recipe.

CATALAN POTATO and BROAD BEAN SOUP

While they are in season fresh broad beans are perfect, but canned or frozen are just as good in this creamy, richly flavoured soup.

SERVES 6

30ml/2 tbsp olive oil
2 onions, chopped
3 large floury potatoes, diced
450g/1lb fresh shelled broad
 (fava) beans
1.75 litres/3 pints/7½ cups vegetable or
 chicken stock
1 bunch coriander (cilantro),
 finely chopped
150ml/¼ pint/⅔ cup single (light) cream
salt and ground black pepper
coriander (cilantro) leaves, to garnish

COOK'S TIP
Broad beans sometimes have a tough outer skin, particularly if they are large. To remove this, first cook the beans briefly in boiling water, then peel off the skin, and add the tender, bright green centre part to the soup.

1 Heat the olive oil in a large pan, add the chopped onions and fry, stirring occasionally with a wooden spoon, for about 5 minutes until they are just softened but not brown.

2 Add the diced potatoes, shelled broad beans (reserving a few for garnishing) and vegetable or chicken stock to the pan. Bring to the boil, then simmer for 5 minutes.

3 Stir in the finely chopped coriander and simmer for a further 10 minutes.

4 Process the soup in batches in a food processor or blender, then return the soup to the rinsed-out pan.

5 Stir in the cream (reserving a little for garnishing), season, and bring to a simmer. Serve garnished with more coriander leaves, beans and cream.

SPANISH POTATO and GARLIC SOUP

Traditionally served in shallow earthenware dishes, this delicious, classic Spanish soup is a great choice for vegetarians.

SERVES 6

30ml/2 tbsp olive oil
1 large onion, finely sliced
4 garlic cloves, crushed
1 large potato, halved and cut
 into thin slices
5ml/1 tsp paprika
400g/14oz can chopped tomatoes, drained
5ml/1 tsp thyme leaves, plus extra chopped
 thyme leaves, to garnish
900ml/1½ pints/3¾ cups vegetable stock
5ml/1 tsp cornflour (cornstarch)
salt and ground black pepper

COOK'S TIP
Paprika is a popular spice in many Spanish dishes. It is made from red peppers that are dried and powdered into a coarse-grained spice. It has a slightly sweet, mild flavour and a rich red colour.

1 Heat the oil in a large, heavy pan, add the onion, garlic, potato and paprika and cook, stirring occasionally, for about 5 minutes, or until the onions have softened, but not browned.

2 Add the chopped tomatoes, thyme leaves and vegetable stock to the pan and simmer for 15–20 minutes until the potatoes have cooked through.

3 In a small bowl, mix the cornflour with a little water to form a smooth paste, then stir into the soup. Bring to the boil, stirring, then simmer for about 5 minutes until the soup has thickened.

4 Using a wooden spoon, break up the potatoes slightly, then season to taste. Serve the soup garnished with the extra chopped thyme leaves.

CORN and POTATO CHOWDER

This creamy yet chunky soup is rich with the sweet taste of corn. It's excellent served with thick, crusty bread and topped with some grated Cheddar cheese.

2 Heat until the oil and butter are sizzling, then reduce the heat to low. Cover the pan and cook gently for about 10 minutes until the vegetables are just softened, shaking the pan occasionally.

3 Pour in the stock, season with salt and pepper to taste and bring to the boil. Reduce the heat, cover the pan again and simmer gently, stirring occasionally, for about 15 minutes, or until the vegetables are tender.

SERVES 4

1 onion, chopped
1 garlic clove, crushed
1 medium baking potato, chopped
2 celery sticks, sliced
1 green (bell) pepper, seeded and sliced
30ml/2 tbsp sunflower oil
25g/1oz/2 tbsp butter
600ml/1 pint/2½ cups vegetable stock
300ml/½ pint/1¼ cups milk
200g/7oz can flageolet, cannellini or haricot (navy) beans
300g/11oz can corn kernels
good pinch of dried sage
salt and ground black pepper
freshly grated Cheddar cheese, to serve

1 Put the onion, garlic, potato, celery and green pepper into a large, heavy pan with the sunflower oil and butter.

4 Add the milk, canned beans and corn kernels – including their liquids. Stir in the dried sage and simmer, uncovered, for 5 minutes, then check the seasoning and adjust to taste. Serve hot in bowls, sprinkled with the grated Cheddar cheese.

CLAM, MUSHROOM and POTATO CHOWDER

The delicate, sweet taste of clams and the soft earthiness of wild mushrooms combine with potatoes to make this a great meal on its own – fit for any occasion.

SERVES 4

48 clams, scrubbed
50g/2oz/¼ cup unsalted (sweet) butter
1 large onion, chopped
1 celery stick, sliced
1 carrot, sliced
225g/8oz assorted wild and cultivated mushrooms
225g/8oz floury potatoes, thickly sliced
1.2 litres/2 pints/5 cups boiling light chicken or vegetable stock
1 thyme sprig
4 parsley stalks
salt and ground black pepper
thyme sprigs, to garnish

1 Place the clams in a large, heavy pan, discarding any that are open. Add 1cm/½in of water to the pan, then cover and bring to the boil. Cook over a medium heat for 6–8 minutes, shaking the pan occasionally, until the clams open (discard any clams that do not open).

2 Drain the clams over a bowl and remove most of the shells, leaving some in the shells as a garnish. Strain the cooking juices into the bowl, add all the clams and set aside.

3 Add the butter, onion, celery and carrot to the pan and cook gently until softened but not coloured. Add the mushrooms and cook for 3–4 minutes until their juices begin to appear. Add the potato slices, the clams and their juices, the stock, thyme and parsley stalks.

4 Bring to the boil, then reduce the heat, cover and simmer for 25 minutes. Season to taste, ladle into soup bowls, and garnish with thyme sprigs.

CHICKEN and LEEK SOUP with PRUNES and BARLEY

This recipe is based on the traditional Scottish soup, Cock-a-leekie. The unusual combination of leeks and prunes is surprisingly delicious.

SERVES 6

115g/4oz/⅔ cup pearl barley
1 chicken, weighing about 2kg/4¼lb
900g/2lb leeks
1 fresh bay leaf
a few fresh parsley stalks and thyme sprigs
1 large carrot, thickly sliced
2.4 litres/4 pints/10 cups chicken or beef stock
400g/14oz ready-to-eat prunes
salt and ground black pepper
chopped fresh parsley, to garnish

1 Rinse the pearl barley thoroughly in a sieve under cold running water, then cook it in a large pan of boiling water for about 10 minutes. Drain the barley, rinse well again and drain thoroughly. Set aside in a cool place.

2 Cut the breast portions off the chicken and set aside, then place the remaining chicken carcass in the pan. Cut half the leeks into 5cm/2in lengths and add them to the pan. Tie the herbs together into a bouquet garni and add to the pan with the carrot and stock.

3 Bring the stock to the boil, then reduce the heat and cover the pan. Simmer gently for 1 hour. Skim off any scum when the water first starts to boil and occasionally during simmering.

4 Add the chicken breast portions to the pan and continue to cook for another 30 minutes until they are just cooked. Leave until cool enough to handle, then strain the stock. Reserve the chicken breast portions and the meat from the carcass. Discard all the skin, bones, cooked vegetables and herbs. Skim as much fat as you can from the stock, then return it to the pan.

5 Add the pearl barley to the stock. Bring to the boil over a medium heat, then lower the heat and cook very gently for 15–20 minutes, until the barley is just cooked and tender. Season the soup with 5ml/1 tsp each salt and ground black pepper.

6 Add the ready-to-eat prunes to the pan, then thinly slice the remaining leeks and add them to the pan. Bring to the boil, then cover the pan and simmer gently for about 10 minutes, or until the leeks are just cooked.

7 Slice the chicken breast portions and then add them to the soup with the remaining chicken meat from the carcass, sliced or cut into neat pieces. Reheat the soup, if necessary, then ladle it into warm, deep soup plates and sprinkle with plenty of chopped parsley to serve.

COCONUT and SEAFOOD SOUP with GARLIC CHIVES

The long list of ingredients in this Thai-inspired recipe could mislead you into thinking that this soup is complicated. In fact, it is very easy to put together.

SERVES 4

600ml/1 pint/2½ cups fish stock
5 thin slices fresh root ginger
2 lemon grass stalks, chopped
3 kaffir lime leaves, shredded
25g/1oz garlic chives (1 bunch), chopped
15g/½oz fresh coriander (cilantro)
15ml/1 tbsp vegetable oil
4 shallots, chopped
400ml/14fl oz can coconut milk
30–45ml/2–3 tbsp Thai fish sauce
45–60ml/3–4 tbsp Thai green curry paste
450g/1lb uncooked large prawns (jumbo shrimp), peeled and deveined
450g/1lb prepared squid
a little lime juice (optional)
salt and ground black pepper
60ml/4 tbsp fried shallot slices, to serve

1 Pour the stock into a pan and add the slices of fresh ginger, the chopped lemon grass and half the lime leaves.

2 Add half the chopped chives to the pan with the coriander stalks. Bring to the boil, then reduce the heat. Cover the pan, then simmer gently for 20 minutes. Strain the stock.

3 Rinse the pan, then add the oil and shallots. Cook over a medium heat for 5–10 minutes, stirring occasionally, until the shallots are just beginning to brown. Stir in the stock, coconut milk, the remaining lime leaves and half the fish sauce. Heat gently until the soup is just simmering and cook over a low heat for 5–10 minutes.

4 Stir in the curry paste and the peeled prawns and cook for 3 minutes. Add the squid, cook for a further 2 minutes. Add the lime juice, if using, and season.

5 Stir in the remaining fish sauce, chopped chives and the chopped coriander leaves. Serve in warmed, shallow bowls sprinkled with fried shallots.

VARIATIONS
• Instead of squid, you could add 400g/14oz firm white fish, such as monkfish, cut into small pieces.
• You could also replace the squid with fresh mussels. Steam 675g/1½lb closed mussels in a tightly covered pan for about 3 minutes, or until the shells have opened. Discard any that remain shut, then remove the mussels from their shells.

MEAT AND GAME

This chapter lifts the lid on delicious main courses made effortlessly in one pot. You'll be reminded of old favourites like Pot-roast Loin of Pork with Apple and Irish Stew, and invited to try some exciting new flavours, such as Minted Lamb Stir-fry, Marinated Pigeon in Red Wine, or Grouse with Orchard Fruit Stuffing. For a wonderful experience you'll be sure to repeat, try Pancetta and Broad Bean Risotto or Spiced Lamb with Tomatoes and Peppers, or a rich Fillet of Beef Stroganoff.

POT-ROAST LOIN of PORK with APPLE

Roasted pork loin with crisp crackling and a lightly spiced apple and raisin stuffing makes a wonderful Sunday-lunch main course.

SERVES 6–8

1.8kg/4lb boned loin of pork
300ml/½ pint/1¼ cups dry (hard) cider
150ml/¼ pint/⅔ cup sour cream
7.5ml/1½ tsp salt

For the stuffing
25g/1oz/2 tbsp butter
1 small onion, chopped
50g/2oz/1 cup fresh white breadcrumbs
2 apples, cored, peeled and chopped
50g/2oz/scant ½ cup raisins
finely grated rind of 1 orange
pinch of ground cloves
salt and ground black pepper

1 Preheat the oven to 220°C/425°F/Gas 7. To make the stuffing, melt the butter in a frying pan and gently fry the onion for 10 minutes until soft. Stir in the remaining stuffing ingredients.

2 Put the pork, rind side down, on a board. Make a horizontal cut between the meat and outer layer of fat, cutting to within 2.5cm/1in of the edges to make a pocket.

3 Push the prepared stuffing into the pocket. Roll up the pork lengthwise and tie firmly with string. Score the rind at 2cm/¾in intervals with a sharp knife.

4 Pour the cider and sour cream into a large casserole. Stir to combine, then add the pork, rind-side down. Transfer to the oven and cook, uncovered, for 30 minutes.

5 Turn the joint over, so that the rind is on top. Baste with the juices, then sprinkle the rind with salt. Cook for a further 1 hour, basting after 30 minutes. Reduce the oven temperature to 180°C/350°F/Gas 4. Cook for 1½ hours, then remove the casserole from the oven and leave the joint to stand for 20 minutes before carving.

COOK'S TIP
Do not baste during the final 1½ hours of roasting, so the crackling becomes crisp.

NOISETTES of PORK with CREAMY CALVADOS and APPLE SAUCE

This dish gives the impression of being far more difficult to prepare than it really is, so it is ideal as part of a formal menu to impress guests. Buttered gnocchi or griddled polenta and red cabbage are suitable accompaniments.

SERVES 4

30ml/2 tbsp plain (all-purpose) flour
4 noisettes of pork, about 175g/6oz each, firmly tied
25g/1oz/2 tbsp butter
4 baby leeks, finely sliced
5ml/1 tsp mustard seeds, coarsely crushed
30ml/2 tbsp Calvados
150ml/¼ pint/⅔ cup dry white wine
2 eating apples, peeled, cored and sliced
150ml/¼ pint/⅔ cup double (heavy) cream
30ml/2 tbsp chopped fresh flat leaf parsley
salt and ground black pepper

1 Place the flour in a bowl and add plenty of seasoning. Turn the noisettes in the flour mixture to coat them lightly.

2 Melt the butter in a heavy frying pan and cook the noisettes until golden on both sides. Remove from the pan and set aside.

3 Add the leeks to the fat remaining in the pan and cook for 5 minutes. Stir in the mustard seeds and pour in the Calvados, then carefully ignite it to burn off the alcohol. When the flames have died down, pour in the wine and replace the pork. Cook gently for 10 minutes, turning the pork frequently.

4 Add the sliced apples to the pan and pour in the cream. Simmer for about 5 minutes, or until the apples are tender and the sauce is thick and creamy. Taste for seasoning, then stir in the chopped fresh parsley and serve immediately.

PANCETTA and BROAD BEAN RISOTTO

This delicious risotto makes a healthy and filling meal, when served with a mixed green salad. Use smoked bacon instead of pancetta, if you like.

SERVES 4

225g/8oz frozen baby broad (fava) beans
15ml/1 tbsp olive oil
1 onion, chopped
2 garlic cloves, finely chopped
175g/6oz smoked pancetta, diced
350g/12oz/1¾ cups risotto rice
1.2 litres/2 pints/5 cups chicken stock
30ml/2 tbsp chopped fresh mixed herbs, such as parsley, thyme and oregano
salt and ground black pepper
coarsely chopped fresh parsley, to garnish
shavings of Parmesan cheese, to serve (see Cook's Tip)

1 First, cook the broad beans in a large flameproof casserole of lightly salted boiling water for about 3 minutes until tender. Drain and set aside.

2 Heat the olive oil in the casserole. Add the chopped onion, chopped garlic and diced pancetta and cook gently for about 5 minutes, stirring occasionally.

3 Add the rice to the pan and cook for 1 minute, stirring. Add 300ml/½ pint/1¼ cups of the stock and simmer, stirring frequently until it has been absorbed.

4 Continue adding the stock, a ladleful at a time, stirring frequently until the rice is just tender and creamy, and almost all of the liquid has been absorbed. This will take 30–35 minutes. It may not be necessary to add all the stock.

5 Stir the beans, mixed herbs and seasoning into the risotto. Heat gently, then serve garnished with the chopped fresh parsley and sprinkled with shavings of Parmesan cheese.

COOK'S TIP
To make thin Parmesan cheese shavings, take a rectangular block or long wedge of Parmesan and firmly scrape a vegetable peeler down the side of the cheese to make shavings. The swivel-bladed type of peeler is best for this job.

SPICED LAMB with TOMATOES and PEPPERS

Select lean tender lamb from the leg for this lightly spiced curry with juicy peppers and wedges of onion. Serve warm naan bread to mop up the tomato-rich juices.

3 Cut two of the onions into wedges (six from each onion) and add to the oil remaining in the pan. Fry the onions over a medium heat for 10 minutes, or until they are beginning to colour. Add the peppers and cook for 5 minutes. Use a slotted spoon to remove the vegetables from the pan and set aside.

4 Meanwhile, chop the remaining onion. Add it to the oil remaining in the pan with the chopped garlic, chilli and ginger, and cook for 4–5 minutes, stirring frequently, until the onion has softened.

5 Stir in the curry paste and canned tomatoes with the reserved yogurt. Return the lamb to the pan, season and stir well. Bring to the boil, then reduce the heat and simmer for 30 minutes.

SERVES 6

1.5kg/3¼lb lean boneless lamb, cubed
250ml/8fl oz/1 cup natural (plain) yogurt
30ml/2 tbsp sunflower oil
3 onions
2 red (bell) peppers, seeded and cut into chunks
3 garlic cloves, finely chopped
1 red chilli, seeded and chopped
2.5cm/1in piece fresh root ginger, peeled and chopped
30ml/2 tbsp mild curry paste
2 × 400g/14oz cans chopped tomatoes
large pinch of saffron threads
800g/1¾lb plum tomatoes, halved, seeded and cut into chunks
salt and ground black pepper
chopped fresh coriander (cilantro), to garnish

1 Mix the lamb with the yogurt in a bowl. Cover and chill for about 1 hour.

2 Heat the oil in a large pan. Drain the lamb and reserve the yogurt, then cook the lamb in batches until it is golden on all sides – this will take about 15 minutes in total. Remove the lamb from the pan using a slotted spoon and set aside.

6 Pound the saffron to a powder in a mortar, then stir in a little boiling water to dissolve the saffron. Add this liquid to the curry and stir well. Return the onion and pepper mixture to the pan, then stir in the fresh tomatoes. Bring the curry back to simmering point and cook for 15 minutes. Garnish with chopped fresh coriander to serve.

MINTED LAMB STIR-FRY

Lamb and mint have a long-established partnership that works particularly well in this full-flavoured stir-fry. Serve with plenty of crusty bread.

SERVES 2

275g/10oz lamb neck fillet or boneless leg steaks
30ml/2 tbsp sunflower oil
10ml/2 tsp sesame oil
1 onion, roughly chopped
2 garlic cloves, crushed
1 red chilli, seeded and finely chopped
75g/3oz fine green beans, halved
225g/8oz fresh spinach, shredded
30ml/2 tbsp oyster sauce
30ml/2 tbsp Thai fish sauce (*nam pla*)
15ml/1 tbsp lemon juice
5ml/1 tsp sugar
45ml/3 tbsp chopped fresh mint
salt and ground black pepper
mint sprigs, to garnish
noodles or rice, to serve

1 Trim the lamb of any excess fat and cut into thin slices. Heat the sunflower and sesame oils in a wok or large frying pan and cook the lamb over a high heat until browned. Remove with a slotted spoon and drain on kitchen paper.

2 Add the onion, garlic and chilli to the wok, cook for 2–3 minutes, then add the beans and stir-fry for 3 minutes.

3 Stir in the shredded spinach with the browned meat, oyster sauce, Thai fish sauce, lemon juice and sugar. Stir-fry for a further 3–4 minutes, or until the lamb is cooked through.

4 Sprinkle in the chopped mint and toss lightly, then adjust the seasoning. Serve piping hot, garnished with mint sprigs and accompanied by noodles or rice.

MIDDLE-EASTERN ROAST LAMB and POTATOES

When the Eastern aroma of the garlic and saffron comes wafting out of the oven, this deliciously garlicky lamb won't last very long.

SERVES 6–8

2.75kg/6lb leg of lamb
4 garlic cloves, halved
60ml/4 tbsp olive oil
juice of 1 lemon
2–3 saffron threads, soaked in 15ml/1 tbsp boiling water
5ml/1 tsp mixed dried herbs, oregano or marjoram
450g/1lb small baking potatoes, thickly sliced
2 large or 4 small onions, thickly sliced
salt and ground black pepper
fresh thyme, to garnish

1 Make eight evenly spaced incisions in the leg of lamb, press the halved garlic cloves into the slits and place the lamb in a large non-metallic dish.

2 Mix together the olive oil, lemon juice, saffron mixture and herbs. Rub over the lamb and marinate for 2 hours.

3 Preheat the oven to 180°C/350°F/Gas 4. Layer the potato and onion slices in a large roasting pan. Lift the lamb out of the marinade and place it on top of the sliced potato and onions, fat side up and season well with plenty of salt and ground black pepper.

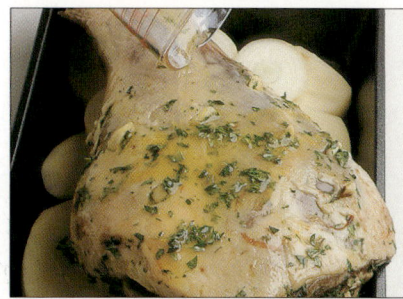

4 Pour the marinade over the lamb, then roast for 2 hours, basting occasionally. Remove from the oven and cover with foil, then rest for 10 minutes before carving. Garnish with thyme.

IRISH STEW

Simple and delicious, this is the quintessential Irish main course. Traditionally, mutton chops are used, but as they are harder to find these days you can use lamb instead.

SERVES 4

1.3kg/3lb boneless lamb chops, cut into large chunks
15ml/1 tbsp vegetable oil
3 onions
4 large carrots
900ml/1½ pints/3¾ cups water
4 large potatoes, cut into large chunks
1 large fresh thyme sprig
15g/½oz/1 tbsp unsalted (sweet) butter
15ml/1 tbsp chopped fresh parsley
salt and ground black pepper

1 Trim any fat from the lamb. Heat the oil in a large, flameproof casserole and brown the meat on all sides. Remove from the casserole.

2 Cut the onions into quarters and thickly slice the carrots. Add them to the casserole and cook for 5 minutes, stirring, or until the onions are browned. Return the meat to the pan with the water. Bring to the boil, reduce the heat, cover and simmer for 1 hour.

3 Add the potatoes to the pan with the thyme and cook for a further 1 hour.

4 Leave the stew to settle for a few minutes. Remove the fat from the liquid with a spoon, then stir in the butter and the parsley. Season well before serving.

POT-ROAST BEEF with GUINNESS

This heart-warming, rich pot-roast is ideal for a winter supper. Brisket of beef has the best flavour but this dish works equally well with rolled silverside or topside.

SERVES 6

30ml/2 tbsp vegetable oil
900g/2lb rolled brisket of beef
275g/10oz onions, roughly chopped
2 celery sticks, thickly sliced
450g/1lb carrots, cut into large chunks
675g/1½lb potatoes, peeled and cut into large chunks
30ml/2 tbsp plain (all-purpose) flour
475ml/16fl oz/2 cups beef stock
300ml/½ pint/1¼ cups Guinness
1 bay leaf
45ml/3 tbsp chopped fresh thyme
5ml/1 tsp soft light brown sugar
30ml/2 tbsp wholegrain mustard
15ml/1 tbsp tomato purée (paste)
salt and ground black pepper

1 Preheat the oven to 180°C/350°F/Gas 4. Heat the oil in a large flameproof casserole and brown the meat all over until golden.

3 Add the celery, carrot and potato to the casserole and cook over a medium heat for 2–3 minutes, or until they are just beginning to colour.

5 Add the bay leaf, thyme, sugar, mustard, tomato purée and plenty of seasoning. Place the meat on top, cover tightly and transfer to the oven.

2 Remove the meat from the pan and drain it on a double layer of kitchen paper. Add the chopped onions to the pan and cook for about 4 minutes, or until they are just beginning to soften and turn brown, stirring all the time.

4 Stir in the flour and cook for a further 1 minute stirring continuously. Pour in the beef stock and the Guinness and stir until well combined. Bring the sauce to the boil, stirring continuously with a wooden spoon.

6 Cook for about 2½ hours, or until the vegetables and meat are tender. Adjust the seasoning and add another pinch of sugar, if necessary. To serve, remove the meat and carve into thick slices. Serve with the vegetables and plenty of gravy.

FILLET of BEEF STROGANOFF

Legend has it that this Russian recipe was devised by Count Paul Stroganov's cook to use beef frozen by the Siberian climate. The only way that it could be prepared was cut into very thin strips. The strips of lean beef were served in a brandy-flavoured cream sauce.

SERVES 8

1.2kg/2½lb beef fillet (tenderloin)
30ml/2 tbsp plain (all-purpose) flour
large pinch each of cayenne pepper and paprika
75ml/5 tbsp sunflower oil
1 large onion, chopped
3 garlic cloves, finely chopped
450g/1lb/6½ cups chestnut mushrooms, sliced
75ml/5 tbsp brandy
300ml/½ pint/1¼ cups beef stock or consommé
300ml/½ pint/1¼ cups sour cream
45ml/3 tbsp chopped fresh flat leaf parsley
salt and ground black pepper

1 Thinly slice the beef fillet across the grain, then cut it into fine strips. Season the flour with the cayenne and paprika.

2 Heat half the oil in a large frying pan and add the chopped onion and garlic.

3 Cook the onion and garlic over a low heat, stirring occasionally until the onion has softened. Add the mushrooms and stir-fry over a high heat for 1–2 minutes. Transfer the vegetables and their juices to a dish and set aside.

4 Wipe the pan, then add and heat the remaining oil. Coat a batch of meat with flour, then fry over a high heat until well browned. Remove from the pan, then coat and fry another batch. When the last batch is cooked, replace all the meat and vegetables. Add the brandy and simmer until it has almost evaporated.

5 Stir in the beef stock or consommé and seasoning and cook for 10–15 minutes, stirring frequently with a wooden spoon, or until the meat is tender and the sauce is thick and glossy. Add the sour cream, stir well and sprinkle with the chopped fresh flat leaf parsley. Serve immediately with plain boiled rice and a simple salad.

COOK'S TIP
If you do not have a very large frying pan, it may be easier to cook this dish in a large, flameproof casserole.

VENISON SAUSAGES with RED WINE GRAVY

Strongly flavoured, meaty sausages are delicious with a robust red wine gravy flavoured with assertive shiitake mushrooms. Serve with soft polenta, mashed potatoes or plenty of thickly sliced crusty bread to mop up the delicious gravy.

SERVES 4

15ml/1 tbsp sunflower oil (optional)
12 venison or wild boar sausages
2 leeks, sliced
2 plump garlic cloves, sliced
225g/8oz/3 cups shiitake
  mushrooms, quartered
15ml/1 tbsp plain (all-purpose) flour
600ml/1 pint/2½ cups red wine
30ml/2 tbsp chopped mixed fresh herbs,
  such as flat leaf parsley and marjoram
salt and ground black pepper

1 Pour the sunflower oil, if using, into a large frying pan, add the venison or wild boar sausages and cook over a medium heat for 15–20 minutes, turning frequently.

2 Add the leeks, garlic and mushrooms and mix well. Cook the vegetables for 10–15 minutes, or until the leeks are soft and beginning to brown.

3 Sprinkle in the flour and gradually pour in the red wine, stirring with a wooden spoon and pushing the sausages around to mix the flour and the liquid smoothly with the leeks.

4 Bring slowly to the boil, reduce the heat and simmer for 10–15 minutes, stirring occasionally, or until the gravy is smooth and glossy. Season the gravy with salt and pepper to taste and then sprinkle the mixed herbs over the sausages. Serve immediately with polenta or mashed potatoes.

COOK'S TIP
Shiitake mushrooms have a slightly floury-looking medium to dark grey-brown cap. They have a firm and meaty texture that becomes silky when cooked. The stalks can be tough so discard if necessary.

GROUSE with ORCHARD FRUIT STUFFING

Tart apples, plums and pears make a fabulous orchard fruit stuffing that complements the rich gamey flavour of grouse perfectly.

SERVES 2

juice of ½ lemon
2 young grouse
50g/2oz/¼ cup butter
4 Swiss chard leaves
50ml/2fl oz/¼ cup Marsala
salt and ground black pepper

For the stuffing
2 shallots, finely chopped
1 tart cooking apple, peeled, cored and chopped
1 pear, peeled, cored and chopped
2 plums, halved, stoned (pitted) and chopped
large pinch of mixed (apple pie) spice

1 Sprinkle the lemon juice over the grouse and season well. Melt half the butter in a flameproof casserole, add the grouse and cook for 10 minutes, or until browned. Use tongs to remove the grouse from the casserole and set aside.

2 Add the shallots to the fat remaining in the casserole and cook until softened but not coloured. Add the apple, pear, plums and mixed spice, and cook for about 5 minutes, or until the fruits are just beginning to soften. Remove the casserole from the heat and spoon the hot fruit mixture into the body cavities of the birds.

3 Truss the birds neatly with string. Smear the remaining butter over the birds and wrap them in the chard leaves, then replace them in the casserole.

4 Pour in the Marsala and heat until simmering. Cover tightly and simmer for 20 minutes, or until the birds are tender, taking care not to overcook them. Leave to rest in a warm place for about 10 minutes before serving.

COOK'S TIP
There isn't a lot of liquid in the casserole for cooking the birds – they are steamed rather than boiled, so it is very important that the casserole has a heavy base and a tight-fitting lid, otherwise the liquid may evaporate and the chard will burn on the base of the pan.

MARINATED PIGEON in RED WINE

The time taken to marinate and cook this casserole is well rewarded by the fabulous rich flavour of the finished dish. Stir-fried green cabbage and celeriac purée are delicious accompaniments to this casserole.

SERVES 4

4 pigeons (US squabs), about 225g/ 8oz each
30ml/2 tbsp olive oil
1 onion, coarsely chopped
225g/8oz/3¼ cups chestnut mushrooms, sliced
15ml/1 tbsp plain (all-purpose) flour
300ml/½ pint/1¼ cups game stock
30ml/2 tbsp chopped fresh parsley
salt and ground black pepper
flat leaf parsley, to garnish

For the marinade
15ml/1 tbsp light olive oil
1 onion, chopped
1 carrot, peeled and chopped
1 celery stick, chopped
3 garlic cloves, sliced
6 allspice berries, bruised
2 bay leaves
8 black peppercorns, bruised
150ml/¼ pint/⅔ cup red wine vinegar
150ml/¼ pint/⅔ cup red wine
45ml/3 tbsp redcurrant jelly

1 Mix together all the ingredients for the marinade in a large bowl. Add the pigeons and turn them in the marinade, then cover the bowl and chill for about 12 hours, turning the pigeons frequently.

VARIATIONS
If you are unable to buy pigeon, this recipe works equally well with chicken or rabbit. Buy portions and make deep slashes in the flesh so that the marinade soaks into, and flavours right to, the centre of the pieces of meat.

2 Preheat the oven to 150°C/300°F/ Gas 2. Heat the oil in a large, flameproof casserole and cook the onion and mushrooms for about 5 minutes, or until the onion has softened.

3 Meanwhile, drain the pigeons and strain the marinade into a jug (pitcher), then set both aside separately.

4 Sprinkle the flour over the pigeons and add them to the casserole, breast-sides down. Pour in the marinade and stock, and add the chopped parsley and seasoning. Cover and cook for 2½ hours.

5 Check the seasoning, then serve the pigeons on warmed plates and ladle the sauce over them. Garnish with parsley.

CHICKEN AND POULTRY

Chicken and duck are perfect ingredients for cooking in one pot and there is nothing better than succulent poultry that has been cooked in the same pot as fresh herbs and vegetables or rice. For an unforgettable taste sensation, you could try mouthwatering Mediterranean Duck with Harissa and Saffron or Chicken Baked with Shallots, Garlic and Fennel. Equally delicious are those dishes that include rice such as Chicken and Prawn Jambalaya, or creamy Risotto with Chicken.

CHICKEN CASSEROLE with WINTER VEGETABLES

A casserole of wonderfully tender chicken, root vegetables and lentils, finished with crème fraîche, mustard and tarragon.

SERVES 4

350g/12oz onions
350g/12oz leeks
225g/8oz carrots
450g/1lb swede (rutabaga)
30ml/2 tbsp oil
4 chicken portions, about 900g/2lb total weight
115g/4oz/½ cup green lentils
475ml/16fl oz/2 cups chicken stock
300ml/½ pint/1¼ cups apple juice
10ml/2 tsp cornflour (cornstarch)
45ml/3 tbsp crème fraîche
10ml/2 tsp wholegrain mustard
30ml/2 tbsp chopped fresh tarragon
salt and ground black pepper
fresh tarragon sprigs, to garnish

1 Preheat the oven to 190°C/375°F/Gas 5. Prepare the onions, leeks, carrots and swede and roughly chop them.

COOK'S TIP
Chop the vegetables into similarly sized pieces so that they cook evenly.

2 Heat the oil in a large flameproof casserole. Season the chicken portions with plenty of salt and pepper and brown them in the hot oil until golden. Drain on kitchen paper.

3 Add the onions to the casserole and cook for 5 minutes, stirring, until they begin to soften and colour. Add the leeks, carrots, swede and lentils to the casserole and stir over a medium heat for 2 minutes.

4 Return the chicken to the pan, then add the stock, apple juice and seasoning. Bring to the boil and cover tightly. Cook in the oven for 50–60 minutes, or until the chicken and lentils are tender.

5 Place the casserole on the stove-top over a medium heat. In a small bowl, blend the cornflour with about 30ml/2 tbsp water to make a smooth paste and add to the casserole with the crème fraîche, wholegrain mustard and chopped tarragon. Adjust the seasoning, then simmer gently for about 2 minutes, stirring, until thickened slightly, before serving, garnished with tarragon sprigs.

COQ au VIN

This French country casserole was traditionally made with an old boiling bird, marinated overnight in red wine, then simmered gently until tender. Modern recipes use tender roasting birds to save time and because boiling fowl are not readily available.

SERVES 6

45ml/3 tbsp light olive oil
12 shallots
225g/8oz rindless streaky (fatty) bacon rashers (strips), chopped
3 garlic cloves, finely chopped
225g/8oz small mushrooms, halved
6 boneless chicken thighs
3 boneless chicken breast portions, halved
1 bottle red wine
salt and ground black pepper
45ml/3 tbsp chopped fresh parsley, to garnish

For the bouquet garni
3 sprigs each parsley, thyme and sage
1 bay leaf
4 peppercorns

For the beurre manié
25g/1oz/2 tbsp butter, softened
25g/1oz/¼ cup plain (all-purpose) flour

1 Heat the oil in a large, flameproof casserole and cook the shallots for about 5 minutes, or until golden. Increase the heat, then add the chopped bacon, garlic and mushrooms and cook for a further 10 minutes, stirring frequently.

2 Use a slotted spoon to transfer the cooked ingredients to a plate, then brown the chicken portions in the oil remaining in the pan, turning them until they are golden brown all over. Return the cooked shallots, garlic, mushrooms and bacon to the casserole and pour in the red wine.

3 Tie the ingredients for the bouquet garni in a bundle in a small piece of muslin (cheesecloth) and add to the casserole. Bring to the boil, reduce the heat and cover the casserole with a tightly fitting lid, then simmer for 30–40 minutes.

4 To make the beurre manié, cream the butter and flour together in a small bowl using your fingers or a spoon to make a smooth paste.

5 Add small lumps of the beurre manié paste to the bubbling casserole, stirring well until each piece has melted into the liquid before adding the next. When all the paste has been added, bring the casserole back to the boil and simmer for 5 minutes.

6 Season the casserole to taste with salt and pepper and serve garnished with chopped fresh parsley and accompanied by boiled potatoes.

CHICKEN BAKED with SHALLOTS, GARLIC and FENNEL

This is a very simple and delicious way to cook chicken. If you have time, leave the chicken to marinate for a few hours for the best flavour.

SERVES 4

1.6–1.8kg/3½–4lb chicken, cut into 8 pieces, or 8 chicken joints
250g/9oz shallots, peeled
1 head of garlic, separated into cloves and peeled
60ml/4 tbsp extra virgin olive oil
45ml/3 tbsp tarragon vinegar
45ml/3 tbsp white wine or vermouth (optional)
5ml/1 tsp fennel seeds, crushed
2 bulbs fennel, cut into wedges, feathery tops reserved
150ml/¼ pint/⅔ cup double (heavy) cream
5ml/1 tsp redcurrant jelly
15ml/1 tbsp tarragon mustard
a little sugar (optional)
30ml/2 tbsp chopped fresh flat leaf parsley
salt and ground black pepper

1 Place the chicken pieces, shallots and all but one of the garlic cloves in a large, shallow flameproof dish. Add the olive oil, tarragon vinegar, white wine or vermouth, if using, and the crushed fennel seeds. Season to taste with plenty of ground black pepper, then set aside and leave to marinate in a cool place for 2–3 hours.

2 Preheat the oven to 190°C/375°F/Gas 5. Add the wedges of fennel to the chicken, then season with salt and stir well to mix. Transfer the chicken to the oven and cook for 50–60 minutes, stirring once or twice, until the chicken is thoroughly cooked. The chicken juices should run clear, not pink, when the thick thigh meat is pierced with a skewer or a small sharp knife.

3 Transfer the chicken and vegetables to a serving dish and keep them warm. Skim off some of the fat and bring the cooking juices to the boil, then pour in the cream. Stir, scraping up all the juices. Whisk in the redcurrant jelly followed by the mustard. Check the seasoning, adding a little sugar, if necessary.

4 Finely chop the remaining garlic clove with the feathery fennel tops and mix them with the parsley. Pour the sauce over the chicken and then sprinkle the chopped garlic and herb mixture over the top. Serve immediately with rice or baked potatoes.

COOK'S TIPS

• If possible, use the fresh, new season's garlic for this dish, as it is plump, moist and full of flavour. Purple-skinned garlic is considered by many cooks to have the best flavour.
• The cut surfaces of fennel will quickly discolour, so do not prepare it too far in advance of using it. If you must prepare it beforehand, then put the wedges into a bowl of cold water acidulated with a little lemon juice.

SEVILLE CHICKEN

Oranges and almonds are favourite ingredients in southern Spain, especially around Seville, where the orange and almond trees are a familiar and wonderful sight.

SERVES 4

1 orange
8 chicken thighs
plain (all-purpose) flour, seasoned with salt and pepper
45ml/3 tbsp olive oil
1 large Spanish onion, roughly chopped
2 garlic cloves, crushed
1 red (bell) pepper, seeded and sliced
1 yellow (bell) pepper, seeded and sliced
115g/4oz chorizo, sliced
50g/2oz/½ cup flaked (sliced) almonds
225g/8oz/generous 1 cup brown basmati rice
about 600ml/1 pint/2½ cups chicken or vegetable stock
400g/14oz can chopped tomatoes
175ml/6fl oz/¾ cup white wine
generous pinch of dried thyme
salt and ground black pepper
fresh thyme sprigs, to garnish

1 Pare a thin strip of peel from the orange using a vegetable peeler and set it aside. Peel the orange, then cut it into even segments, working over a bowl to catch any excess juice. Dust the chicken thighs with plenty of seasoned flour.

2 Heat the olive oil in a large frying pan and fry the chicken pieces on both sides until nicely brown. Transfer the browned chicken to a plate. Add the chopped onion and crushed garlic to the pan and fry for 4–5 minutes until the onion begins to brown. Add the sliced red and yellow peppers to the pan and fry, stirring occasionally with a wooden spoon, until they are slightly softened.

3 Add the chorizo, stir-fry for a few minutes, then sprinkle over the almonds and rice. Cook, stirring, for 1–2 minutes.

4 Pour in the chicken or vegetable stock, chopped tomatoes and white wine, then add the reserved orange peel and the dried thyme. Season well. Bring the sauce to simmering point, stirring, then return the chicken to the pan.

5 Cover tightly and cook over a very low heat for 1–1¼ hours until the rice and chicken are tender. Just before serving, add the orange segments and juice, and allow to cook briefly to heat through. Season to taste, garnish with sprigs of fresh thyme and serve.

CHICKEN with CHICKPEAS and ALMONDS

The almonds in this tasty Moroccan-style recipe are pre-cooked until soft, adding an interesting texture and flavour to the chicken.

SERVES 4

75g/3oz/½ cup blanched almonds
75g/3oz/½ cup chickpeas, soaked overnight and drained
4 part-boned chicken breast portions, skinned
50g/2oz/4 tbsp butter
2.5ml/½ tsp saffron threads
2 Spanish onions, finely sliced
900ml/1½ pints/3¾ cups chicken stock
1 small cinnamon stick
60ml/4 tbsp chopped fresh flat leaf parsley, plus extra to garnish
lemon juice, to taste
salt and ground black pepper

1 Place the blanched almonds and the soaked and drained chickpeas in a large flameproof casserole of water and bring to the boil. Boil for 10 minutes, then reduce the heat. Simmer for 1–1½ hours until the chickpeas are soft. Drain the chickpeas and almonds and set aside.

2 Place the skinned chicken pieces in the casserole, together with the butter, half of the saffron, and salt and plenty of black pepper. Heat gently, stirring, until the butter has melted.

3 Add the onions and stock, bring to the boil, then add the reserved cooked almonds, chickpeas and cinnamon stick. Cover with a tightly fitting lid and cook very gently for 45–60 minutes until the chicken is completely tender.

4 Transfer the cooked chicken to a serving plate and keep warm. Bring the sauce to the boil and cook over a high heat until it is well reduced, stirring frequently with a wooden spoon.

5 Add the chopped parsley and remaining saffron to the casserole and cook for a further 2–3 minutes. Sharpen the sauce with a little lemon juice, then pour the sauce over the chicken and serve, garnished with extra fresh parsley.

CHICKEN with TOMATOES and HONEY

A thick tomato and honey sauce coats chicken pieces in this subtly spiced dish.

SERVES 4

30ml/2 tbsp sunflower oil
25g/1oz/2 tbsp butter
4 chicken quarters
1 onion, grated or very finely chopped
1 garlic clove, crushed
5ml/1 tsp ground cinnamon
good pinch of ground ginger
1.3–1.6kg/3–3½lb tomatoes, peeled, cored and roughly chopped
30ml/2 tbsp clear honey
50g/2oz/⅓ cup blanched almonds
15ml/1 tbsp sesame seeds
salt and ground black pepper
chopped flat leaf parsley, to garnish

1 Place the oil and butter in a large, flameproof casserole. Add the chicken and cook over a medium heat for about 3 minutes until it is lightly browned.

2 Add the grated or chopped onion, garlic, cinnamon, ginger, tomatoes and plenty of seasoning, and heat gently until the tomatoes begin to bubble.

3 Lower the heat and then cover the casserole. Simmer very gently for about 1 hour, stirring and turning the chicken occasionally, or until it is completely cooked through.

4 Lift out the chicken pieces and transfer them to a plate. Increase the heat and cook the tomato sauce until it is reduced to a thick purée, stirring frequently. Stir in the honey, cook for 1 minute, then return the chicken pieces to the pan and cook for 2–3 minutes to heat through.

5 Transfer the chicken and sauce to a warmed serving dish and sprinkle with the blanched almonds and sesame seeds. Serve hot, garnished with parsley.

COOK'S TIP
To blanch whole almonds, place them in a strainer and lower it into boiling water. Cook the almonds for 2–3 minutes, then remove the strainer from the water. Pinch the softened almond skin between your thumb and finger to squeeze it off.

CHICKEN with FORTY CLOVES of GARLIC

This dish does not have to be mathematically exact, so do not worry if you have 35 or even 50 cloves of garlic – the important thing is that there should be lots. The smell that emanates from the oven as the chicken and garlic cook is indescribably delicious.

SERVES 4–5

5–6 whole heads of garlic
15g/½oz/1 tbsp butter
45ml/3 tbsp olive oil
1.8–2kg/4–4½lb chicken
150g/5oz/1¼ cups plain (all-purpose) flour, plus 5ml/1 tsp
75ml/5 tbsp white port, Pineau de Charentes or other white, fortified wine
2–3 fresh tarragon or rosemary sprigs
30ml/2 tbsp crème fraîche (optional)
a few drops of lemon juice (optional)
salt and ground black pepper

1 Separate three of the heads of garlic into cloves and peel them. Remove the first layer of papery skin from the remaining heads of garlic and cut off the tops to expose the cloves, if you like, or leave them whole. Preheat the oven to 180°C/350°F/Gas 4.

2 Heat the butter and 15ml/1 tbsp of the olive oil in a flameproof casserole that is just large enough to take the chicken and garlic. Add the chicken and cook over a medium heat, turning it frequently, for 10–15 minutes, until it is browned all over.

3 Sprinkle in 5ml/1 tsp flour and cook for 1 minute. Add the port or wine. Tuck in the whole heads of garlic and the peeled cloves with the sprigs of tarragon or rosemary. Pour over the remaining oil and season to taste with salt and pepper.

4 Mix the main batch of flour with sufficient water to make a firm dough. Roll it out into a long sausage and press it around the rim of the casserole, then press on the lid, folding the dough up and over it to create a tight seal. Cook in the oven for 1½ hours.

5 To serve, lift off the lid to break the seal and remove the chicken and whole garlic to a serving platter and keep warm. Remove and discard the herb sprigs, then place the casserole on the stove top and whisk the remaining ingredients to combine the garlic cloves with the juices. Add the crème fraîche, if using, and a little lemon juice to taste, if using. Process the sauce in a food processor or blender until smooth. Reheat the garlic sauce in a clean pan if necessary and serve it with the chicken.

CHICKEN BIRIANI

Easy to make and very tasty, this is the ideal one-pot dish for a family supper.

SERVES 4

10 green cardamom pods
275g/10oz/1½ cups basmati rice, soaked and drained
2.5ml/½ tsp salt
2–3 cloves
5cm/2in cinnamon stick
45ml/3 tbsp vegetable oil
3 onions, sliced
4 chicken breast portions, each about 175g/6oz, cubed
1.5ml/¼ tsp ground cloves
5ml/1 tsp ground cumin
5ml/1 tsp ground coriander
2.5ml/½ tsp ground black pepper
3 garlic cloves, chopped
5ml/1 tsp finely chopped fresh root ginger
juice of 1 lemon
4 tomatoes, sliced
30ml/2 tbsp chopped fresh coriander (cilantro)
150ml/¼ pint/⅔ cup natural (plain) yogurt
4–5 saffron threads, soaked in 10ml/2 tsp hot milk
150ml/¼ pint/⅔ cup water
toasted flaked (sliced) almonds and fresh coriander (cilantro) sprigs, to garnish
natural (plain) yogurt, to serve

1 Preheat the oven to 190°C/375°F/Gas 5. Remove the seeds from half the cardamom pods and grind them finely, using a mortar and pestle. Set the seeds aside.

2 Bring a flameproof casserole of water to the boil and add the soaked and drained basmati rice, then stir in the salt, the remaining whole cardamom pods, whole cloves and cinnamon stick. Boil the rice for 2 minutes, then drain, leaving the whole spices in the rice.

3 Heat the oil in the flameproof casserole and fry the onions for about 8 minutes, until softened and browned. Add the cubed chicken and the ground spices, including the ground cardamom seeds. Mix well, then add the chopped garlic, ginger and lemon juice. Stir-fry the mixture together for 5 minutes.

4 Arrange the sliced tomatoes on top. Sprinkle on the coriander, spoon the yogurt on top and cover with the rice.

5 Drizzle the saffron milk over the rice and add the water. Cover and bake for 1 hour. Garnish with almonds and coriander and serve with extra yogurt.

CHICKEN and PRAWN JAMBALAYA

This colourful mixture of rice, peppers and tomatoes with chicken, gammon and prawns is flavoured with garlic and fresh herbs and a few dashes of fiery Tabasco sauce. It's an ideal dish for big family gatherings and celebrations.

SERVES 10

2 chickens, each about 1.3–1.6kg/3–3½lb
450g/1lb piece raw smoked gammon (smoked or cured ham)
50g/2oz/⅓ cup lard or bacon fat
50g/2oz/½ cup plain (all-purpose) flour
3 onions, finely sliced
2 green (bell) peppers, seeded and sliced
675g/1½lb tomatoes, peeled and chopped
2–3 garlic cloves, crushed
10ml/2 tsp chopped fresh thyme or 5ml/1 tsp dried thyme
24 raw Mediterranean prawns (jumbo shrimp), peeled with tails intact
500g/1¼lb/2½ cups white long grain rice
1.2 litres/2 pints/5 cups water
2–3 dashes Tabasco sauce
45ml/3 tbsp chopped fresh flat leaf parsley, plus tiny fresh parsley sprigs to garnish
salt and ground black pepper

1 Cut each chicken into ten pieces and season the pieces well with salt and pepper. Dice the gammon, discarding the rind and fat.

2 Melt the lard or bacon fat in a large, heavy frying pan. Add the chicken pieces in several batches, cook them until they are golden brown all over, then lift them out with a slotted spoon and set them aside.

3 Reduce the heat. Sprinkle the flour into the fat in the pan and stir with a wooden spoon until the roux turns a golden brown colour. Return the chicken pieces to the pan.

4 Add the diced gammon, onions, green peppers, tomatoes, garlic and thyme and stir well to mix. Cook, stirring regularly, for about 10 minutes, then add the prawns and mix lightly.

5 Stir the rice into the frying pan and pour in the water. Season well with salt, black pepper and Tabasco sauce. Bring to the boil, then cook gently, stirring occasionally, until the rice is tender and all the liquid has been fully absorbed. Add a little extra boiling water if the rice looks like drying out before it is cooked. Check the seasoning and add salt, pepper and more Tabasco if necessary.

6 Mix the chopped fresh flat leaf parsley into the finished dish, garnish with tiny sprigs of flat leaf parsley and serve the jambalaya immediately with plenty of crusty bread.

RISOTTO with CHICKEN

This is a classic risotto combination of creamy rice and tender cubes of chicken, flavoured with aromatic saffron, prosciutto, white wine and Parmesan cheese.

SERVES 6

30ml/2 tbsp olive oil
225g/8oz skinless, boneless chicken breast portions, cut into 2.5cm/1in cubes
1 onion, finely chopped
1 garlic clove, finely chopped
450g/1lb/2¼ cups risotto rice
120ml/4fl oz/½ cup dry white wine
1.5ml/¼ tsp saffron threads
1.75 litres/3 pints/7½ cups simmering chicken stock
50g/2oz prosciutto, cut into thin strips
25g/1oz/2 tbsp butter, diced
25g/1oz/⅓ cup freshly grated Parmesan cheese, plus extra to serve
salt and ground black pepper
sprigs of flat leaf parsley, to garnish

1 Heat the olive oil in a large frying pan over a medium-high heat. Add the cubes of chicken and cook, stirring occasionally with a wooden spoon, until they start to turn white.

2 Reduce the heat to low and add the chopped onion and garlic. Cook, stirring occasionally, until the onion is soft. Stir in the risotto rice, then sauté for 2 minutes, stirring constantly, until all the rice grains are coated in oil.

3 Add the dry white wine to the rice mixture and cook, stirring constantly, until the wine has been absorbed. Add the saffron threads to the simmering stock and stir well, then add ladlefuls of hot stock to the rice mixture, allowing each ladleful to be fully absorbed before adding the next.

4 When the rice is about three-quarters cooked, add the strips of prosciutto and stir well. Continue cooking, stirring occasionally, until the rice is just tender and the risotto is creamy.

5 Add the butter and the Parmesan and stir in well. Season with salt and pepper to taste. Serve the risotto hot, sprinkled with a little more Parmesan, and garnish with flat leaf parsley.

STIR-FRIED CRISPY DUCK

This stir-fry would be delicious wrapped in flour tortillas or steamed Chinese pancakes, with a little extra warm plum sauce.

2 Heat the oil in a wok or large frying pan and cook the duck over a high heat until golden and crisp. Keep stirring to prevent the duck from sticking. Remove the duck with a slotted spoon and drain on kitchen paper. You may need to cook the duck in several batches.

3 Add the spring onions to the pan and cook for 2 minutes. Stir in the cabbage and cook for 5 minutes, or until it is softened and golden.

SERVES 2

275–350g/10–12oz boneless duck breast
30ml/2 tbsp plain (all-purpose) flour
60ml/4 tbsp oil
1 bunch spring onions (scallions), halved lengthwise and cut into 5cm/2in strips, plus extra to garnish
275g/10oz/2½ cups finely shredded green cabbage
225g/8oz can water chestnuts, drained and sliced
50g/2oz/½ cup unsalted cashew nuts
115g/4oz cucumber, cut into strips
45ml/3 tbsp plum sauce
15ml/1 tbsp light soy sauce
salt and ground black pepper

1 Remove any skin from the duck breast, then trim off a little of the fat. Thinly slice the meat into even-size pieces. Season the flour with plenty of salt and pepper and use it to completely coat each piece of duck.

4 Return the duck to the pan with the water chestnuts, cashews and cucumber. Stir-fry for 2 minutes. Add the plum sauce and soy sauce and season to taste, then heat for 2 minutes. Serve garnished with the sliced spring onions.

MEDITERRANEAN DUCK with HARISSA and SAFFRON

Harissa is a fiery chilli sauce from north Africa. Mixed with cinnamon, saffron and preserved lemon, it gives this colourful casserole an unforgettable flavour.

SERVES 4

15ml/1 tbsp olive oil
1.8–2kg/4–4½lb duck, quartered
1 large onion, thinly sliced
1 garlic clove, crushed
2.5ml/½ tsp ground cumin
400ml/14fl oz/1⅔ cups duck or
    chicken stock
juice of ½ lemon
5–10ml/1–2 tsp harissa
1 cinnamon stick
5ml/1 tsp saffron threads
50g/2oz/⅓ cup black olives
50g/2oz/⅓ cup green olives
peel of 1 preserved lemon, rinsed, drained
    and cut into fine strips
2–3 lemon slices
30ml/2 tbsp chopped fresh coriander
    (cilantro), plus extra leaves
    to garnish
salt and ground black pepper

1 Heat the oil in a flameproof casserole. Add the duck quarters and cook until browned all over. Remove the duck with a slotted spoon and set aside. Add the onion and garlic to the oil remaining in the casserole and cook for 5 minutes until soft. Add the ground cumin and cook, stirring, for 2 minutes.

COOK'S TIP
The term "duck" refers to birds over two months old. The rich flavour of duck is best appreciated when a duck reaches its full-grown size. Look for a duck with a supple, waxy skin with a dry appearance. It should have a long body with tender, meaty breasts.

2 Pour in the stock and lemon juice, then add the harissa, cinnamon and saffron. Bring to the boil. Return the duck to the casserole and add the olives, preserved lemon peel and lemon slices. Season with salt and pepper.

3 Lower the heat, partially cover the casserole and simmer gently for about 45 minutes, or until the duck is cooked through. Discard the cinnamon stick. Stir in the chopped coriander and garnish with the coriander leaves.

FISH AND SHELLFISH

For a simple, healthy meal with superb flavour, fish and shellfish are the perfect choice for one-pot cooking. Baked Sea Bream with Tomatoes would make a fine dish for a mid-week family meal, Seafood Risotto is a good choice for an impromptu supper with friends, while for a more formal dinner you could try something unusual such as Gingered Seafood Stir-fry, Fish with Fregola, Moroccan Fish Tagine or a never-fail colourful Seafood Paella.

TUNA FRITTATA

This is the ultimate meal in a pan – easy to prepare and easy to serve. For a stronger cheese flavour, try a creamy goat's cheese in place of the soft white cheese.

SERVES 2–3

25g/1oz/2 tbsp butter
15ml/1 tbsp olive oil
1 onion, finely chopped
175g/6oz courgettes (zucchini), halved lengthwise and sliced
75g/3oz/1¼ cups brown cap (cremini) mushrooms, sliced
50g/2oz asparagus tips
4 eggs, beaten
75g/3oz/⅜ cup soft white (farmer's) cheese or ricotta cheese
30ml/2 tbsp chopped fresh thyme
200g/7oz can tuna, in olive oil, drained and roughly flaked
115g/4oz cooked, peeled prawns (shrimp)
salt and ground black pepper

1 Heat the butter and oil in a non-stick frying pan. Add the chopped onion and cook for 3 minutes, then add the sliced courgettes, mushrooms and asparagus tips and cook for a further 10 minutes, or until beginning to soften and brown.

2 Beat together the eggs, soft or ricotta cheese, chopped thyme and plenty of seasoning until they are well combined.

3 Stir the tuna into the pan, add the prawns and season well. Heat through gently. Pour over the egg mixture and cook over a gentle heat for 5 minutes.

4 Push the egg away from the sides to allow the uncooked egg to run on to the pan. Preheat the grill (broiler) to medium and grill (broil) the omelette to set and brown the surface. Serve cut in wedges.

FILLETS of BRILL in RED WINE SAUCE

Forget the old maxim that red wine and fish do not go well together. The robust sauce adds colour and richness to this excellent dish, which is more than elegant enough for a dinner party. Halibut and John Dory are also good cooked this way.

SERVES 4

4 fillets of brill, about 175–200g/6–7oz each, skinned
150g/5oz/10 tbsp chilled butter, diced, plus extra for greasing
115g/4oz shallots, thinly sliced
200ml/7fl oz/scant 1 cup robust red wine
200ml/7fl oz/scant 1 cup fish stock
salt and ground black and white pepper
fresh flat leaf parsley leaves or chervil, to garnish

1 Preheat the oven to 180°C/350°F/Gas 4. Season the fish fillets on both sides with salt and ground black pepper. Generously butter a shallow flameproof dish, which is large enough to take all the brill fillets in a single layer. Spread the shallots in an even layer in the dish and lay the fish fillets on top. Season well with salt and ground black pepper.

2 Pour in the red wine and fish stock, cover the dish with a lid or foil and then bring the liquid to just below boiling point. Transfer the dish to the oven and bake for 6–8 minutes, or until the brill is just cooked.

3 Using a fish slice (metal spatula), lift the fish and shallots on to a serving dish, cover with foil and keep hot.

4 Transfer the dish to the stove and bring the cooking liquid to the boil over a high heat. Cook it until it has reduced by half. Lower the heat and whisk in the chilled butter, one piece at a time, to make a smooth, shiny sauce. Season with salt and ground white pepper, set the sauce aside and keep hot.

5 Divide the shallots among four warmed plates and lay the brill fillets on top. Pour the sauce over and around the fish and garnish with the fresh flat leaf parsley or chervil.

BAKED SEA BREAM with TOMATOES

John Dory, halibut or sea bass can all be cooked this way. If you prefer to use filleted fish, choose a chunky fillet, such as cod, and roast it skin-side up. Roasting the tomatoes brings out their sweetness, which contrasts beautifully with the flavour of the fish.

SERVES 4–6

8 ripe tomatoes
10ml/2 tsp sugar
200ml/7fl oz/scant 1 cup olive oil
450g/1lb new potatoes
1 lemon, sliced
1 bay leaf
1 fresh thyme sprig
8 fresh basil leaves
1 sea bream, about 900g–1kg/2–2¼lb, cleaned and scaled
150ml/¼ pint/⅔ cup dry white wine
30ml/2 tbsp fresh white breadcrumbs
2 garlic cloves, crushed
15ml/1 tbsp finely chopped fresh parsley
salt and ground black pepper
fresh flat parsley or basil leaves, chopped, to garnish

1 Preheat the oven to 240°C/475°F/Gas 9. Cut the tomatoes in half lengthwise and arrange them in a single layer in a baking dish, cut-side up. Sprinkle with sugar, salt and pepper and drizzle over a little of the olive oil. Roast for 30–40 minutes, until lightly browned. Remove the tomatoes from the dish and set aside.

2 Meanwhile, cut the potatoes into 1cm/½in slices. Place in a large pan of salted water and par-boil for 5 minutes. Drain and set aside.

3 Grease the baking dish with a little more of the oil. Arrange the potatoes in a single layer with the lemon slices over; sprinkle on the herbs. Season and drizzle with half the remaining oil. Lay the fish on top and season. Pour over the wine and the rest of the oil. Arrange the tomatoes around the fish.

4 Mix together the breadcrumbs, garlic and parsley; sprinkle over the fish. Bake for 30 minutes. Garnish with chopped parsley or basil.

FISH with FREGOLA

This Sardinian speciality is a cross between a soup and a stew. Serve it with crusty Italian country bread to mop up the juices.

SERVES 4–6

75ml/5 tbsp olive oil
4 garlic cloves, finely chopped
½ small fresh red chilli, seeded and finely chopped
1 large handful fresh flat leaf parsley, roughly chopped
1 red snapper, about 450g/1lb, cleaned, with head and tail removed
1 grey mullet or porgy, about 500g/1¼lb, cleaned, with head and tail removed
350–450g/12oz–1lb thick cod fillet
400g/14oz can chopped plum tomatoes
175g/6oz/1½ cups dried fregola
250ml/8fl oz/1 cup water
salt and ground black pepper

1 Heat 30ml/2 tbsp of the olive oil in a large flameproof casserole. Add the chopped garlic and chilli, with about half the chopped fresh parsley. Fry over a medium heat, stirring occasionally, for about 5 minutes.

2 Cut all of the fish into large chunks – including the skin and the bones in the case of the snapper and mullet – and add the pieces to the casserole. Sprinkle with a further 30ml/2 tbsp of the olive oil and fry for a few minutes more.

3 Add the tomatoes, then fill the empty can with water and add to the pan. Bring to the boil. Season to taste, lower the heat and cook for 10 minutes.

4 Add the fregola and simmer for about 5 minutes, then add the water and the remaining oil. Simmer for 15 minutes until the fregola is just tender.

5 If the sauce becomes too thick, add more water, then taste for seasoning. Serve hot, in warmed bowls, sprinkled with the remaining parsley.

VARIATION
Any white fish fillet can be used instead of cod in this dish. Monkfish, haddock, hake or plaice could all be used.

COOK'S TIPS
• Fregola is a tiny pasta shape from Sardinia. If you can't get it, use a tiny soup pasta (*pastina*), such as *corallini* or *semi de melone*.
• You can make the basic fish sauce several hours in advance or even the day before, bringing it to the boil and adding the fregola just before serving.

FISH PLAKI

Greece has so much coastline, it's no wonder that fish is so popular there. Generally, it is treated simply, but in this recipe the fish is cooked with onions and tomatoes.

SERVES 6

300ml/½ pint/1¼ cups olive oil
2 onions, thinly sliced
3 large, well-flavoured tomatoes, roughly chopped
3 garlic cloves, thinly sliced
5ml/1 tsp sugar
5ml/1 tsp chopped fresh dill
5ml/1 tsp chopped fresh mint
5ml/1 tsp chopped fresh celery leaves
15ml/1 tbsp chopped fresh flat leaf parsley
300ml/½ pint/1¼ cups water
6 hake or cod steaks
juice of 1 lemon
salt and ground black pepper
extra fresh dill, mint or parsley sprigs, to garnish

1 Heat the oil in large heavy sauté pan or flameproof casserole. Add the onions and cook, stirring, until pale golden, then add the tomatoes, garlic, sugar, dill, mint, celery leaves and parsley with the water. Season with salt and pepper, then simmer, uncovered, for 25 minutes, until the liquid has reduced by one-third.

2 Add the fish steaks and cook gently for 10–12 minutes until the fish is just cooked. Remove the pan or casserole from the heat and add the lemon juice. Cover and leave to stand for 20 minutes before serving. Arrange the cod in a dish and pour the sauce over. Garnish with herbs and serve warm or cold.

MOROCCAN FISH TAGINE

This spicy, aromatic dish proves just how exciting an ingredient fish can be. Serve it with couscous, which you can steam in the traditional way in a colander on top of the tagine.

SERVES 8

1.3kg/3lb firm fish fillets, skinned and cut into 5cm/2in chunks
60ml/4 tbsp olive oil
1 large aubergine (eggplant), cut into 1cm/½in cubes
2 courgettes (zucchini), cut into 1cm/½in cubes
4 onions, chopped
400g/14oz can chopped tomatoes
400ml/14fl oz/1⅔ cups passata (bottled strained tomatoes)
200ml/7fl oz/scant 1 cup fish stock
1 preserved lemon, chopped
90g/3½oz/scant 1 cup olives
60ml/4 tbsp chopped fresh coriander (cilantro), plus extra coriander leaves to garnish
salt and ground black pepper

For the harissa
3 large fresh red chillies, seeded and chopped
3 garlic cloves, peeled
15ml/1 tbsp ground coriander
30ml/2 tbsp ground cumin
5ml/1 tsp ground cinnamon
grated rind of 1 lemon
30ml/2 tbsp sunflower oil

1 Make the harissa. Whizz everything in a food processor to a smooth paste.

2 Put the fish in a wide bowl and add 30ml/2 tbsp of the harissa. Toss to coat, cover and chill for at least 1 hour.

COOK'S TIP
To make the fish go further, add 225g/8oz/ 1¼ cups cooked chickpeas to the tagine.

3 Heat half the olive oil in a shallow heavy pan. Add the aubergine cubes and fry for about 10 minutes, or until they are golden brown. Add the courgettes and fry for a further 2 minutes. Remove the vegetables from the pan using a slotted spoon and set aside.

4 Add the remaining olive oil to the pan, add the onions and cook over a low heat for about 10 minutes until golden brown. Stir in the remaining harissa and cook for 5 minutes, stirring occasionally.

5 Add the vegetables and combine with the onions, then stir in the chopped tomatoes, the passata and fish stock. Bring to the boil, then lower the heat and simmer for about 20 minutes.

6 Stir the fish chunks and preserved lemon into the pan. Add the olives and stir gently. Cover and simmer over a low heat for about 15–20 minutes. Season to taste. Stir in the chopped coriander. Serve with couscous, if you like, and garnish with coriander leaves.

COD and PRAWN GREEN COCONUT CURRY

This quick curry takes just minutes to make. If you can't find green masala curry paste at your local supermarket, simply substitute another variety – the curry will be just as good.

SERVES 4

675g/1½lb cod fillets, skinned
90ml/6 tbsp green masala curry paste
175ml/6fl oz/¾ cup canned coconut milk or 200ml/7fl oz/scant 1 cup coconut cream
175g/6oz raw or cooked, peeled prawns (shrimp)
fresh coriander (cilantro), to garnish
basmati rice, to serve

VARIATION
Any firm fish, such as monkfish, can be used instead of cod. Whole fish steaks can be cooked in the sauce, but allow an extra 5 minutes' cooking time and baste them with the sauce from time to time.

1 Using a sharp knife, cut the skinned cod fillets into 4cm/1½in pieces.

2 Put the green masala curry paste and the coconut milk or cream into a frying pan. Heat to simmering and simmer gently for 5 minutes, stirring occasionally.

3 Add the cod pieces and prawns (if raw) to the cream mixture and cook gently for 5 minutes. If using cooked prawns, then add them after this time and heat through. Garnish the curry with fresh coriander and serve immediately with basmati rice.

FISH STEW with LEMON GRASS

Lemon grass and ginger give this delicate stew of fish, prawns, new potatoes and broccoli an appetizing aromatic flavour.

SERVES 4

25g/1oz/2 tbsp butter
175g/6oz onions, chopped
20ml/4 tsp plain (all-purpose) flour
400ml/14fl oz/1⅔ cups light fish stock
150ml/¼ pint/⅔ cup white wine
2.5cm/1in piece fresh root ginger, peeled and finely chopped
2 lemon grass stalks, trimmed and finely chopped
450g/1lb new potatoes, scrubbed and halved if necessary
450g/1lb white fish fillets
175g/6oz large, cooked, peeled prawns (shrimp)
275g/10oz small broccoli florets
150ml/¼ pint/⅔ cup double (heavy) cream
60ml/4 tbsp chopped fresh garlic chives
salt and ground black pepper
crusty bread, to serve

1 Melt the butter in a large pan. Add the onions and cook for 3–4 minutes. Stir in the flour and cook for 1 minute.

2 Stir in the stock, wine, ginger, lemon grass and potatoes. Season and bring to the boil. Cover and cook for 15 minutes, or until the potatoes are almost tender.

3 Remove the skin from the fish fillets and cut the fillets into large chunks. Add the chunks of fish to the pan with the prawns, broccoli and cream. Stir gently.

4 Simmer gently for 5 minutes, taking care not to break up the fish. Adjust the seasoning and sprinkle in the chives. Serve with plenty of crusty bread.

MUSSELS and CLAMS with LEMON GRASS and COCONUT CREAM

Lemon grass has an incomparable flavour and aroma and is widely used in Thai cooking, especially with seafood. If you have difficulty obtaining fresh baby clams for this recipe, then use a few extra mussels instead.

SERVES 6

1.8–2kg/4–4½lb mussels
450g/1lb baby clams
120ml/4fl oz/½ cup dry white wine
1 bunch spring onions (scallions), chopped
2 lemon grass stalks, chopped
6 kaffir lime leaves, chopped
10ml/2 tsp Thai green curry paste
200ml/7fl oz/scant 1 cup coconut cream
30ml/2 tbsp chopped fresh coriander (cilantro)
salt and ground black pepper
garlic chives, to garnish

1 Clean the mussels by pulling off the beards, scrubbing the shells well and removing any barnacles. Discard any broken mussels or any that do not close when tapped sharply. Wash the clams.

COOK'S TIP
The kaffir lime tree is native to Southeast Asia and both the leaves and fruit rind are used in cooking. Dried kaffir lime leaves, available from supermarkets, can be used in place of fresh – add them at the beginning of the cooking time and remove and discard just before serving.

2 Put the white wine in a large, heavy pan with the spring onions, chopped lemon grass stalks, kaffir lime leaves and Thai green curry paste. Simmer all the ingredients together until the wine has almost evaporated.

3 Add the mussels and clams to the pan, cover tightly and steam the shellfish over a high heat for 5–6 minutes, or until they open.

4 Using a slotted spoon, transfer the cooked mussels and clams to a heated serving bowl and keep hot. At this stage discard any shellfish that remain closed. Strain the cooking liquid into the clean pan and gently simmer until it is reduced to about 250ml/8fl oz/1 cup.

5 Stir in the coconut cream and fresh coriander, with plenty of salt and pepper to taste. Increase the heat and simmer gently until the sauce is piping hot. Pour the sauce over the mussels and clams and serve immediately, garnished with garlic chives.

GINGERED SEAFOOD STIR-FRY

This would make a lovely summer supper. Serve with lots of bread to mop up the juices and some chilled dry white wine. It would also be good as a first course for four.

SERVES 2

15ml/1 tbsp sunflower oil
5ml/1 tsp sesame oil
2.5cm/1in piece fresh root ginger, peeled and finely chopped
1 bunch spring onions (scallions), sliced
1 red (bell) pepper, seeded and finely chopped
115g/4oz small "queen" scallops
8 large, raw prawns (shrimp), peeled
115g/4oz squid rings
15ml/1 tbsp lime juice
15ml/1 tbsp light soy sauce
60ml/4 tbsp coconut milk
salt and ground black pepper
mixed salad leaves and crusty bread, to serve

1 Heat the sunflower and sesame oils in a wok or large frying pan and cook the chopped ginger and sliced spring onions for 2–3 minutes, stirring frequently, until golden brown. Add the chopped red pepper and cook, stirring constantly, for a further 3 minutes.

2 Add the scallops, prawns and squid rings to the wok or frying pan and cook over a medium heat for about 3 minutes stirring occasionally with a wooden spoon, until all the seafood is opaque and just cooked through. Add the lime juice and light soy sauce.

3 Pour in the coconut milk and mix well, then simmer the sauce, uncovered, for 2 minutes, until the sauce begins to thicken slightly.

4 Season the stir-fry well. Arrange the mixed salad leaves on two individual serving plates and spoon over the seafood mixture with the juices. Serve the seafood with plenty of crusty bread to mop up the juices.

SEAFOOD PAELLA

There are as many versions of paella as there are regions of Spain. Those from near the coast contain a lot of seafood, while inland versions add chicken or pork. Here the only meat is the chorizo – essential for an authentic flavour.

SERVES 4

45ml/3 tbsp olive oil
1 large onion, chopped
2 fat garlic cloves, chopped
150g/5oz chorizo, sliced
300g/11oz small squid, cleaned
1 red (bell) pepper, seeded and sliced
4 tomatoes, peeled, seeded and diced, or 200g/7oz can tomatoes
about 500ml/17fl oz/generous 2 cups chicken stock
105ml/7 tbsp dry white wine
200g/7oz/1 cup short grain Spanish rice or risotto rice
a large pinch of saffron threads
150g/5oz/1¼ cups fresh or frozen peas
12 large cooked prawns (shrimp), in the shell, or 8 langoustines
450g/1lb mussels, scrubbed
450g/1lb clams, scrubbed
salt and ground black pepper

1 Heat the olive oil in a large sauté pan or a paella pan, add the onion and garlic and fry until the onion is translucent. Add the chorizo and fry until golden.

2 If the squid are very small, you can leave them whole; otherwise cut the bodies into rings and the tentacles into pieces. Add the squid to the pan and sauté over a high heat for 2 minutes, stirring occasionally.

3 Stir in the pepper slices and the seeded and diced tomatoes and simmer gently for 5 minutes, until the pepper slices are tender. Pour in the stock and wine, stir well and bring to the boil.

4 Stir in the rice and saffron and season to taste with salt and pepper. Spread the contents of the pan in an even layer over the base. Bring the liquid back to the boil, then lower the heat and simmer gently for 10 minutes.

5 Add the peas, prawns or langoustines, mussels and clams, stirring them gently into the rice. Cook gently for another 15–20 minutes, until the rice is tender and all the mussels and clams have opened. If any remain closed, discard them. If the paella seems dry, add a little more stock. Gently stir everything together and serve piping hot.

Fish and Shellfish **67**

SEAFOOD RISOTTO

Creamy, saffron-flavoured rice makes the perfect foil for shellfish. Ready-prepared, frozen seafood mixtures, which include prawns, squid and mussels, are ideal for making this quick and easy dish – remember to thaw them before cooking.

SERVES 4

1 litre/1¾ pints/4 cups fish or
　shellfish stock
50g/2oz/¼ cup unsalted (sweet) butter
2 shallots, chopped
2 garlic cloves, chopped
350g/12oz/1¾ cups risotto rice
150ml/¼ pint/⅔ cup dry white wine
2.5ml/½ tsp powdered saffron, or a
　pinch of saffron threads
400g/14oz mixed prepared seafood,
　thawed if frozen
30ml/2 tbsp freshly grated
　Parmesan cheese
30ml/2 tbsp chopped fresh flat leaf parsley,
　to garnish
salt and ground black pepper

1 Pour the fish or shellfish stock into a large, heavy pan. Bring it to the boil, then pour it into a large, heatproof jug (pitcher) or bowl and keep warm.

2 Melt the butter in the rinsed-out pan pan, add the shallots and garlic and cook over a low heat for 3–5 minutes, stirring occasionally, until the shallots are soft but not coloured. Add the rice, stir well to coat the grains completely with butter, then pour in the dry white wine. Cook over a medium heat, stirring occasionally, until the wine has been absorbed by the rice.

COOK'S TIP
It is essential to use proper risotto rice, such as arborio or carnaroli, for this dish. It has a wonderfully creamy texture when cooked but still retains a "bite".

3 Add a ladleful of hot stock and the saffron, and cook, stirring continuously, until the liquid has been absorbed. Add the seafood and stir well. Continue to add hot stock a ladleful at a time, waiting until each quantity has been absorbed before adding more. Stir the mixture for about 20 minutes in all until the rice is swollen and creamy, but still with a little bite in the middle.

VARIATION
Use peeled prawns (shrimp), or cubes of fish such as cod or salmon in place of the mixed prepared seafood.

4 Vigorously mix in the freshly grated Parmesan cheese and season to taste, then sprinkle over the chopped parsley and serve immediately.

VEGETARIAN AND PASTA

The great thing about these vegetarian dishes is that many of them are made with ingredients you will almost certainly have in your kitchen, so they are the recipes you'll make time and time again for all the family. Vegetable Korma is very adaptable, and Pasta Twists with Pesto is as easy as its name suggests. For a more unusual taste experience, try Jamaican Black Bean Pot or the delicious Basmati Rice and Nut Pilaff.

FRITTATA with LEEK, RED PEPPER and SPINACH

Apart from the fact that Italian frittata does not usually contain potato and is generally slightly softer in texture, it is not hugely different from Spanish tortilla. This combination of sweet leek, red pepper and spinach is delicious with the egg.

SERVES 3–4

30ml/2 tbsp olive oil
1 large red (bell) pepper, seeded and diced
2.5–5ml/½–1 tsp ground cumin
3 leeks (about 450g/1lb), thinly sliced
150g/5oz baby spinach leaves
45ml/3 tbsp pine nuts, toasted
5 large (US extra large) eggs
15ml/1 tbsp chopped fresh basil
15ml/1 tbsp chopped fresh flat leaf parsley
salt and ground black pepper
watercress, to garnish
50g/2oz/⅔ cup freshly grated Parmesan cheese, to serve (optional)

1 Heat a heavy, non-stick frying pan and add the olive oil. Add the diced red pepper and cook over a medium heat, stirring occasionally, for 6–8 minutes, until the pepper is soft and beginning to brown. Add 2.5ml/½ tsp of the ground cumin, mix well and cook for another 1–2 minutes.

2 Stir in the thinly sliced leeks, then partly cover the pan and cook gently for about 5 minutes, or until the leeks have softened and collapsed. Season the cooked vegetables with plenty of salt and ground black pepper.

3 Add the spinach and cover the pan. Allow the spinach to wilt in the steam for 3–4 minutes, then stir to mix it into the vegetables, adding the pine nuts.

4 Beat the eggs with salt, pepper, the remaining cumin, basil and parsley. Add to the pan and cook over a gentle heat until the base of the omelette sets and turns golden brown. Pull the edges of the omelette away from the sides of the pan as it cooks and tilt the pan so that the uncooked egg runs underneath.

5 Preheat the grill (broiler). Flash the frittata under the hot grill to set the egg on top, but do not let it become too brown. Cut the frittata into wedges and serve warm, garnished with watercress and sprinkled with Parmesan, if using.

VARIATION
A delicious way to serve frittata is to pack it into a slightly hollowed-out loaf and then drizzle it with olive oil. Wrap tightly in clear film (plastic wrap) and stand for 1–2 hours before cutting into slices.

NEW POTATOES and VEGETABLES BAKED TURKISH-STYLE

Here's a meal in a pot that's suitable for feeding large numbers of people. It's lightly spiced and has plenty of garlic – who could refuse?

SERVES 4

60ml/4 tbsp olive oil
1 large onion, chopped
2 aubergines (eggplant), cut into small cubes
4 courgettes (zucchini), cut into small chunks
1 green (bell) pepper, seeded and chopped
1 red or yellow (bell) pepper, seeded and chopped
115g/4oz/1 cup fresh or frozen peas
115g/4oz green beans
450g/1lb new or salad potatoes, cubed
2.5ml/½ tsp ground cinnamon
2.5ml/½ tsp ground cumin
5ml/1 tsp paprika
4–5 tomatoes, skinned
400g/14oz can chopped tomatoes
30ml/2 tbsp chopped fresh parsley
3–4 garlic cloves, crushed
350ml/12fl oz/1½ cups vegetable stock
salt and ground black pepper
black olives and fresh parsley, to garnish

1 Preheat the oven to 190°C/375°F/Gas 5. Heat 45ml/3 tbsp of the oil in a large frying pan, add the onion and fry until golden.

2 Add the aubergines and sauté for about 3 minutes, then add the courgettes, chopped peppers, peas, beans and cubed potatoes, together with the cinnamon, cumin, paprika and seasoning. Continue to cook for a further 3 minutes, stirring the mixture constantly. Transfer the vegetables to an ovenproof dish.

3 Halve the fresh tomatoes, remove the seeds using a teaspoon and then chop the tomato flesh. Mix the tomato flesh with the canned tomatoes, chopped parsley, crushed garlic and the remaining olive oil in a bowl.

4 Pour the vegetable stock over the aubergine and pepper mixture and then spoon the prepared tomato mixture evenly over the top. Cover the dish with foil and bake for 30–45 minutes. Serve hot, garnished with olives and parsley.

RATATOUILLE

A highly versatile vegetable stew from Provence. Ratatouille is delicious hot or cold, on its own or with eggs, pasta, fish or meat – particularly roast lamb.

SERVES 6

900g/2lb ripe, well-flavoured tomatoes
120ml/4fl oz/½ cup olive oil
2 onions, thinly sliced
2 red (bell) peppers, seeded and cut into chunks
1 yellow or orange (bell) pepper, seeded and cut into chunks
1 large aubergine (eggplant), cut into chunks
2 courgettes (zucchini), cut into thick slices
4 garlic cloves, crushed
2 bay leaves
15ml/1 tbsp chopped fresh thyme
salt and ground black pepper

1 To skin the tomatoes plunge them into a bowl of boiling water for about 30 seconds, remove them using a slotted spoon and then refresh in cold water. Peel away the skins and roughly chop the tomato flesh.

2 Heat a little of the oil in a large, heavy pan and fry the onions for 5 minutes. Add the peppers and fry for a further 2 minutes. Drain. Add the aubergine and more oil and fry gently for 5 minutes. Add the remaining oil and courgettes and fry for 3 minutes. Drain.

3 Add the garlic and tomatoes to the pan with the bay leaves and thyme and a little salt and pepper. Cook gently until the tomatoes have softened and are turning pulpy.

4 Return all the vegetables to the pan and cook gently, stirring frequently, for about 15 minutes, until they are fairly pulpy but have retained a little texture. Season with more salt and pepper to taste if required.

COOK'S TIPS
• There are no specific quantities for the vegetables when making ratatouille so you can, to a large extent, vary the quantities and types of vegetables depending on what you have in the refrigerator.
• If the tomatoes are a little tasteless, add 30–45ml/2–3 tbsp tomato purée (paste) and a pinch of sugar to the mixture along with the tomatoes.
• Aubergines no longer need to be salted to draw out the bitter juices, however, this salting process does help prevent the aubergines from soaking up too much oil during frying. So, if you have the time, it is worth sprinkling the aubergine chunks with salt and leaving them in a colander in the sink for about 30 minutes to drain. Rinse them well and pat dry with kitchen paper before frying.

OKRA and TOMATO TAGINE

A spicy vegetarian dish that is delicious served either with other vegetable dishes or as a side dish to accompany a meat tagine.

SERVES 4

350g/12oz small okra
5–6 tomatoes
2 small onions
2 garlic cloves, crushed
1 green chilli, seeded
5ml/1 tsp paprika
a small handful of fresh coriander (cilantro) leaves
30ml/2 tbsp vegetable oil
juice of 1 lemon
120ml/4fl oz/½ cup water

1 Preheat the oven to 190°C/350°F/Gas 5. Trim the okra, then cut the pods into 1cm/½in lengths. Set aside.

2 Peel the tomatoes, remove the seeds, then chop roughly. Set aside. Chop one of the onions, place in a food processor with the garlic, spices and 60ml/4 tbsp water and blend to form a paste.

3 Thinly slice the second onion. Heat the oil in a flameproof casserole or pan and fry the onion for 5–6 minutes until it turns golden brown. Transfer to a plate with a slotted spoon.

4 Reduce the heat and pour the onion and coriander paste over the onions. Cook for 1–2 minutes, stirring frequently, then add the okra, tomatoes and lemon juice. Pour in the water and stir well to mix. Cover tightly and transfer to the oven. Bake for about 15 minutes until the okra is tender.

5 Transfer the tagine to a serving dish, sprinkle with the fried onion rings and serve immediately.

VARIATION
Canned, chopped tomatoes can be used instead of the fresh tomatoes in this recipe – simply add the contents of a 200g/7oz can with the okra in step 4.

JAMAICAN BLACK BEAN POT

Molasses imparts a rich treacly flavour to the spicy sauce, which incorporates a stunning mix of black beans, vibrant red and yellow peppers and orange butternut squash.

SERVES 4

225g/8oz/1¼ cups dried black beans
1 bay leaf
30ml/2 tbsp vegetable oil
1 large onion, chopped
1 garlic clove, chopped
5ml/1 tsp mustard powder
15ml/1 tbsp molasses or black treacle
30ml/2 tbsp soft dark brown sugar
5ml/1 tsp dried thyme
2.5ml/½ tsp dried chilli flakes
5ml/1 tsp vegetable bouillon powder
1 red (bell) pepper, seeded and diced
1 yellow (bell) pepper, seeded and diced
675g/1½lb butternut squash or pumpkin, seeded and cut into 1cm/½in dice
salt and ground black pepper
sprigs of thyme, to garnish
cornbread or plain boiled rice, to serve

1 Soak the beans overnight in plenty of water, then drain and rinse well. Place in a large pan, cover with fresh water and add the bay leaf. Bring to the boil, then boil rapidly for 10 minutes. Reduce the heat, cover the pan, and simmer for about 30 minutes until tender. Drain, reserving the cooking water. Preheat the oven to 180°C/350°F/Gas 4.

COOK'S TIPS
• To prepare squash or pumpkin, cut it in half using a large sharp knife, then cut off the skin. Remove the seeds using a spoon and cut the flesh into chunks. Choose firm specimens that are blemish-free.
• If you don't have bouillon powder, then dissolve half a stock (bouillon) cube in the bean cooking water.

2 Heat the vegetable oil in a flameproof casserole, add the onion and garlic and sauté for about 5 minutes until softened, stirring occasionally. Stir in the mustard powder, molasses or treacle, sugar, dried thyme, chilli flakes and seasoning. Cook for about 1 minute, stirring, then stir in the black beans.

3 Add enough water to the reserved liquid to make 400ml/14fl oz/1⅔ cups, mix in the bouillon powder and pour into the casserole. Bake for 25 minutes.

4 Add the peppers and the squash or pumpkin and mix well. Cover, then bake for 45 minutes. Garnish with thyme.

VEGETABLE KORMA

The blending of spices is an ancient art in India. Here the aim is to produce a subtle, aromatic curry rather than an assault on the senses.

SERVES 4

50g/2oz/¼ cup butter
2 onions, sliced
2 garlic cloves, crushed
2.5cm/1in piece fresh root ginger, grated
5ml/1 tsp ground cumin
15ml/1 tbsp ground coriander
6 cardamom pods
5cm/2in piece of cinnamon stick
5ml/1 tsp ground turmeric
1 fresh red chilli, seeded and
　finely chopped
1 potato, peeled and cut into
　2.5cm/1in cubes
1 small aubergine (eggplant), chopped
115g/4oz/1½ cups mushrooms,
　thickly sliced
175ml/6fl oz/¾ cup water
115g/4oz/1 cup green beans, cut into
　2.5cm/1in lengths
60ml/4 tbsp natural (plain) yogurt
150ml/¼ pint/⅔ cup double (heavy) cream
5ml/1 tsp garam masala
salt and ground black pepper
fresh coriander (cilantro) sprigs, to garnish
boiled rice and poppadums, to serve

1 Melt the butter in a heavy pan. Add the onions and cook for 5 minutes until soft. Add the garlic and ginger and cook for 2 minutes, then stir in the cumin, coriander, cardamom pods, cinnamon stick, turmeric and finely chopped chilli. Cook, stirring constantly, for 30 seconds.

2 Add the potato cubes, aubergine and mushrooms and the water. Cover the pan, bring to the boil, then lower the heat and simmer for 15 minutes. Add the beans and cook, uncovered, for 5 minutes. With a slotted spoon, remove the vegetables to a warmed serving dish and keep hot.

3 Allow the cooking liquid to bubble up until it has reduced a little. Season with salt and pepper, then stir in the yogurt, cream and garam masala. Pour the sauce over the vegetables and garnish with fresh coriander. Serve with boiled rice and poppadums.

VARIATION
All kinds of vegetables and pulses can be used for this korma; try broccoli, carrots, cauliflower, peas, canned or fresh beans and canned chickpeas.

BASMATI RICE and NUT PILAFF

Vegetarians will love this simple pilaff. Add wild or cultivated mushrooms, if you like.

SERVES 4

15–30ml/1–2 tbsp sunflower oil
1 onion, chopped
1 garlic clove, crushed
1 large carrot, coarsely grated
225g/8oz/generous 1 cup basmati rice, soaked
5ml/1 tsp cumin seeds
10ml/2 tsp ground coriander
10ml/2 tsp black mustard seeds (optional)
4 green cardamom pods
450ml/¾ pint/scant 2 cups vegetable stock or water
1 bay leaf
75g/3oz/½ cup shelled walnuts and/or unsalted cashew nuts
salt and ground black pepper
fresh parsley or coriander (cilantro) sprigs, to garnish

1 Heat the oil in a large frying pan. Add the onion, garlic and carrot and cook for 3–4 minutes, stirring occasionally.

2 Drain the rice and add it to the pan with the cumin seeds, ground coriander, black mustard seeds, if using, and the green cardamom pods. Cook for about 1 minute, stirring to coat the grains in oil.

3 Pour in the vegetable stock or water, add the bay leaf and season well with salt and pepper. Bring to the boil, then lower the heat, cover and simmer very gently for 10–12 minutes.

4 Remove the frying pan from the heat without lifting the lid. Leave to stand in a warm place for about 5 minutes, then check the rice. If it is cooked, there will be small steam holes on the surface of the rice. Remove the bay leaf and the cardamom pods.

5 Stir the walnuts and/or cashew nuts into the rice mixture. Taste to check the seasoning and add more salt and pepper if necessary. Spoon into warmed individual bowls or on to a large platter, garnish with the sprigs of fresh parsley or coriander and serve immediately.

COOK'S TIPS
• Use whichever nuts you prefer in this pilaff – even unsalted peanuts taste good – although almonds, brazil nuts, cashew nuts or pistachio nuts add a slightly more exotic flavour.
• If you don't have basmati rice, then use any other long grain rice. Thai jasmine rice has a particularly good flavour.

VEGETABLE COUSCOUS with SAFFRON and HARISSA

This spicy, north African dish makes an excellent main meal, or serve as part of a vegetarian buffet.

SERVES 4

45ml/3 tbsp olive oil
1 onion, chopped
2 garlic cloves, crushed
5ml/1 tsp ground cumin
5ml/1 tsp paprika
400g/14oz can chopped tomatoes
300ml/½ pint/1¼ cups vegetable stock
1 cinnamon stick
generous pinch of saffron threads
4 baby aubergines (eggplant), quartered
8 baby courgettes (zucchini), trimmed
8 baby carrots
225g/8oz/1⅓ cups couscous
425g/15oz can chickpeas, drained
175g/6oz/¾ cup pitted prunes
45ml/3 tbsp chopped fresh parsley
45ml/3 tbsp chopped fresh coriander
10–15ml/2–3 tsp harissa
salt

1 Heat the olive oil in a large pan. Add the onion and garlic and cook gently for 5 minutes until soft. Add the cumin and paprika and cook, stirring, for 1 minute.

2 Add the tomatoes, stock, cinnamon stick, saffron, aubergines, courgettes and carrots, and season with salt. Bring to the boil, cover, lower the heat and cook gently for 20 minutes until the vegetables are just tender.

3 Line a steamer or colander with a double thickness of muslin (cheesecloth). Soak the couscous according to the instructions on the packet.

COOK'S TIPS
• Couscous is made from durum wheat and has a similar appearance to semolina. It has a very mild flavour and takes on the flavour of any ingredients it is mixed with. Most couscous is sold pre-cooked and only needs to be re-hydrated in boiling water or according to packet instructions.
• Harissa is a spicy paste made from red chillies, coriander, caraway, garlic, salt and olive oil. Its bright red/orange colour is an indicator of its fiery flavour. It is sold in cans, jars and tubes.

4 Add the chickpeas and prunes to the vegetables, stir and cook for 5 minutes.

5 Spread the couscous in the prepared steamer. Place the steamer on top of the vegetables, cover and cook for 5 minutes until the couscous is hot.

6 Stir the herbs into the vegetables. Heap the couscous on to a serving dish. Using a slotted spoon, remove the vegetables from the frying pan and add to the couscous. Spoon over a little sauce and toss gently. Stir the harissa into the remaining sauce and serve separately.

BUCKWHEAT NOODLES with CABBAGE, POTATOES and CHEESE

This is a very unusual pasta dish from Valtellina in the Italian Alps. The pale brown buckwheat noodles called pizzoccheri are unique to this area.

SERVES 6

400g/14oz Savoy cabbage, cut into 1cm/½in strips
2 potatoes, total weight about 200g/7oz, cut into 5mm/¼in slices
400g/14oz dried pizzoccheri (buckwheat noodles)
75g/3oz/6 tbsp butter
1 generous bunch fresh sage leaves, shredded
2 garlic cloves
200g/7oz Fontina cheese, rind removed and thinly sliced
30–45ml/2–3 tbsp freshly grated Parmesan cheese, plus extra to serve
salt and ground black pepper

COOK'S TIPS
• Look for packets of dried pizzoccheri pasta in Italian delicatessens.
• Fontina is an Italian mountain cheese with a sweet, nutty taste. If you cannot get it, look for Taleggio, Gruyère or Emmenthal – they are all similar cheeses.

1 Bring a very large pan of salted water to the boil. Add the cabbage strips and potato slices and boil for 5 minutes.

2 Add the pasta to the pan, stir well and let the water return to the boil over a high heat. Lower the heat and simmer for about 15 minutes, or according to the instructions on the packet, until the pasta is just tender.

3 Drain the pasta and vegetables and set aside. Melt the butter in the pan. Add the sage and whole garlic cloves and fry over a low to medium heat until the garlic is golden and sizzling. Lift the garlic out of the pan and discard it. Set the sage and garlic butter aside.

4 Pour one-quarter of the pasta and vegetable mixture into a warmed large bowl and arrange about one-third of the Fontina slices on top. Repeat these layers until all the ingredients have been used, then sprinkle with the grated Parmesan. Pour the sage and garlic butter over the top and serve immediately, with extra grated Parmesan handed separately.

VARIATION
You could use chard or spinach instead of the cabbage. Spinach will need much less cooking, so add it to the pan about 5 minutes before the end of the cooking time in step 2.

FETTUCINE with BUTTER and PARMESAN

Very few ingredients are needed to make up this incredibly simple dish. It comes from northern Italy, where butter and cheeses are the most popular ingredients for serving with pasta. This dish is especially popular with children.

SERVES 4

400g/14oz fresh or dried fettucine
50g/2oz/¼ cup unsalted (sweet) butter, cubed
115g/4oz/1¼ cups freshly grated Parmesan cheese
salt and ground black pepper

VARIATIONS
• Other long pastas would be just as good in this recipe; try spaghetti, linguine or tagliatelle. Spinach or tomato flavoured versions would also work well.
• Try freshly grated Pecorino cheese instead of the Parmesan.

1 Cook the pasta in a large pan of salted boiling water until just tender, or according to the instructions on the packet. Drain thoroughly, then tip the pasta into a large warmed bowl.

2 Add the cubes of butter and the grated Parmesan, one-third at a time, tossing the pasta after each addition until it is evenly coated. Season to taste and serve immediately.

PASTA TWISTS with PESTO

Bottled pesto is a useful stand-by, but if you have a food processor or blender, it is very easy to make a delicious home-made version.

SERVES 4

50g/2oz fresh basil leaves, plus extra fresh basil leaves, to garnish
2–4 garlic cloves
60ml/4 tbsp pine nuts
120ml/4fl oz/½ cup extra virgin olive oil
115g/4oz/1¼ cups freshly grated Parmesan cheese, plus extra to serve
25g/1oz/¼ cup freshly grated Pecorino cheese
400g/14oz/3½ cups dried pasta twists (fusilli)
salt and ground black pepper

1 Put the basil, garlic and pine nuts in a food processor. Add 60ml/4 tbsp of the oil. Process until chopped, then stop the machine and scrape the bowl.

2 Turn the machine on again and slowly add the remaining olive oil in a thin, steady stream through the feeder tube. You may need to stop the machine and scrape down the sides of the bowl once or twice to make sure that everything is evenly mixed.

3 Scrape the mixture into a large bowl and beat in the cheeses with a wooden spoon. Taste and add salt and ground black pepper if necessary.

4 Cook the pasta in a large pan of salted boiling water for 10 minutes, or according to the instructions on the packet, until just tender. Drain the pasta well, then add it to the bowl of pesto and toss well. Serve immediately, garnished with the extra fresh basil leaves. Hand around the extra shaved Parmesan separately.

COOK'S TIP
Fresh pesto can be made up to 2–3 days in advance. To store it, transfer the pesto to a small bowl and pour a thin film of olive oil over the surface. Cover the bowl tightly with clear film (plastic wrap) and keep it in the refrigerator.

PASTA SHELLS with TOMATOES and RICOTTA

Nothing could be more simple than hot pasta tossed with fresh ripe tomatoes, ricotta cheese and sweet basil. Serve it on hot summer days – it is surprisingly refreshing.

SERVES 4–6

350g/12oz/3 cups dried conchiglie
130g/4½oz/generous ½ cup ricotta cheese
6 ripe plum tomatoes, diced
2 garlic cloves, crushed
a handful of fresh basil leaves, shredded,
 plus extra basil leaves to garnish
60ml/4 tbsp extra virgin olive oil
salt and ground black pepper

1 Cook the pasta in boiling salted water according to the packet instructions.

VARIATIONS
• Use diced mozzarella instead of ricotta.
• An avocado is the ideal ingredient for adding extra colour and flavour to this pasta dish. Halve, stone (pit) and peel, then dice the flesh. Toss it with the hot pasta at the last minute.

2 Meanwhile, put the ricotta cheese in a large mixing bowl and mash with a fork until soft and creamy.

3 Add the diced tomatoes (see Cook's Tip), crushed garlic and shredded basil to the softened ricotta cheese, with salt and pepper to taste, and mix well. Add the olive oil and whisk thoroughly. Taste for seasoning.

4 Drain the cooked pasta, add it to the ricotta and tomato mixture and toss well to mix. Garnish with basil leaves and serve immediately, sprinkled with black pepper.

COOK'S TIP
If you like, skin the tomatoes before you dice them by plunging them into boiling water for 30 seconds and then refresh in cold water before peeling.

SIDE DISHES

With the modern emphasis on eating plenty of vegetables, serving several side dishes makes sense, but it can present logistical problems. Space on top of the stove is often limited, so use the oven as well. If you want something that's simple to prepare but a little more exciting than plain steamed or boiled vegetables, you'll find Courgettes in Tomato Sauce or Roasted Tomatoes and Garlic are the perfect answer. There are also plenty of recipes here for a special occasion: try Baked Fennel with a Crumb Crust, Spinach with Sweet Potatoes, or Baby Leeks in Red Wine with Aromatics.

BRAISED CARROTS with LEEKS

Sweet carrots and leeks go well together and are good finished with a little chopped mint, chervil or parsley. This is a good accompaniment to roast beef, lamb or chicken.

SERVES 4

65g/2½oz/5 tbsp butter
675g/1½lb carrots, thickly sliced
a little sugar
2 fresh bay leaves
75ml/5 tbsp water
675g/1½lb leeks, cut into 5cm/2in lengths
120ml/4fl oz/½ cup white wine
30ml/2 tbsp chopped fresh mint, chervil or parsley
salt and ground black pepper

1 Melt 25g/1oz/2 tbsp of the butter in a wide, heavy pan and cook the carrots without allowing them to brown, for about 5 minutes. Add the bay leaves, seasoning, sugar and the water. Bring to the boil, cover and cook for 10 minutes, or until the carrots are just tender.

2 Uncover the pan and boil until the juices have evaporated, leaving the carrots moist and glazed. Remove the carrots from the pan and set aside.

3 Melt 25g/1oz/2 tbsp of the remaining butter in the pan. Add the leeks and fry them over a low heat for 4–5 minutes, without allowing them to brown.

4 Add seasoning, a good pinch of sugar, the wine and half the chopped herbs. Heat until simmering, then cover and cook gently for 5–8 minutes, until the leeks are tender, but not collapsed.

5 Uncover the leeks and turn them in the buttery juices. Increase the heat and then boil the liquid rapidly until it is reduced to a few tablespoons.

6 Add the carrots to the leeks and reheat them gently, stirring occasionally, then add the remaining butter. Adjust the seasoning, if necessary. Transfer to a warmed serving dish and serve sprinkled with the remaining chopped herbs.

VARIATION
Braised leeks in tarragon cream
Cook 900g/2lb leeks, cut into 5cm/2in lengths, in 40g/1½oz/3 tbsp butter as step 3. Season with salt and pepper, add a pinch of sugar, 45ml/3 tbsp tarragon vinegar, 6 fresh tarragon sprigs or 5ml/1 tsp dried tarragon and 60ml/4 tbsp white wine. Cover and cook as step 4. Add 150ml/¼ pint/⅔ cup double (heavy) cream and allow to bubble and thicken. Adjust the seasoning and serve sprinkled with plenty of finely chopped fresh tarragon leaves. A spoonful of tarragon-flavoured mustard is good stirred into these creamy leeks. Serve with fish or chicken dishes.

Side Dishes

BABY LEEKS in RED WINE with AROMATICS

Coriander seeds and oregano lend a Greek flavour to this dish of braised leeks. Serve it as part of a mixed hors d'oeuvre or as a partner for baked white fish.

SERVES 6

12 baby leeks or 6 thick leeks
15ml/1 tbsp coriander seeds, lightly crushed
5cm/2in piece of cinnamon stick
120ml/4fl oz/½ cup olive oil
3 fresh bay leaves
2 strips pared orange rind
5–6 fresh or dried oregano sprigs
5ml/1 tsp sugar
150ml/¼ pint/⅔ cup fruity red wine
10ml/2 tsp balsamic or sherry vinegar
30ml/2 tbsp coarsely chopped fresh oregano or marjoram
salt and ground black pepper

1 For baby leeks, simply trim the ends, but leave them whole. If you are using thicker leeks, cut them into 5–7.5cm/2–3in lengths.

2 Place the coriander seeds and cinnamon in a pan wide enough to take all the leeks in a single layer. Cook over a medium heat for 2–3 minutes, until the spices give off a fragrant aroma, then stir in the olive oil, bay leaves, orange rind, fresh or dried oregano, sugar, wine and balsamic or sherry vinegar. Bring to the boil and simmer for 5 minutes.

3 Add the leeks to the pan. Bring back to the boil, reduce the heat and cover the pan. Cook the leeks gently for 5 minutes. Uncover and simmer gently for another 5–8 minutes, until the leeks are just tender when tested with the tip of a sharp knife.

4 Use a slotted spoon to transfer the leeks to a serving dish. Boil the pan juices rapidly until reduced to about 75–90ml/5–6 tbsp. Add salt and pepper to taste and pour the liquid over the leeks. Leave to cool.

5 The leeks can be left to stand for several hours. If you chill them, bring them back to room temperature again before serving. Sprinkle the chopped herbs over the leeks just before serving.

COOK'S TIP
Genuine balsamic vinegar from Modena in northern Italy has been produced for over 1,000 years. It has a high sugar content and wonderfully strong bouquet. It is a very dark brown colour and has a deep, rich flavour with hints of herbs and port. Nowadays you can find quite good balsamic vinegar in supermarkets. It is expensive, but the flavour is so rich that you only need to use a little.

BRAISED LETTUCE and PEAS with MINT

Based on the traditional French way of braising peas with lettuce in butter, this dish is delicious with simply cooked fish or roast or grilled duck.

SERVES 4

50g/2oz/¼ cup butter
4 Little Gem (Bibb) lettuces, halved lengthwise
2 bunches spring onions (scallions)
5ml/1 tsp sugar
400g/14oz shelled peas (about 1kg/2¼lb in pods)
a few sprigs of mint, plus extra fresh mint to garnish
120ml/4fl oz/½ cup light vegetable or chicken stock or water
salt and ground black pepper

1 Melt half the butter in a wide, heavy pan over a low heat. Add the lettuces and spring onions.

2 Toss the vegetables in the butter, then sprinkle in the sugar, 2.5ml/½ tsp salt and plenty of black pepper. Cover, then cook very gently for 5 minutes, stirring once.

3 Add the peas and mint sprigs to the pan. Toss the peas in the buttery juices, then pour in the light stock or water.

4 Cover the pan and cook over a gentle heat for a further 5 minutes until the peas are almost tender, then remove the lid from the pan. Increase the heat to high and cook, stirring occasionally, until the cooking liquid has reduced to a few tablespoons.

5 Stir in the remaining butter and adjust the seasoning. Transfer to a warmed serving dish and garnish with the extra mint. Serve immediately.

VARIATIONS
• Braise about 250g/9oz baby carrots with the lettuce.
• Use 1 lettuce, shredding it coarsely, and omit the fresh mint. Towards the end of cooking, stir in about 150g/5oz rocket (arugula) – preferably the slightly stronger-flavoured, wild variety – and cook briefly until just wilted.
• Fry 115g/4oz chopped smoked bacon or pancetta with 1 small chopped red or white onion in the butter. Use 1 bunch of spring onions and omit the mint. Stir in some chopped fresh flat leaf parsley before serving. This version is also very good with small, white summer turnips, braised with the lettuce.

SPINACH with SWEET POTATOES

Sweet potatoes make an interesting alternative to the ordinary variety. Here the garlic and ginger subtly complement the flavours of the potatoes and spinach.

SERVES 4

30ml/2 tbsp sunflower oil
1 onion, chopped
1 garlic clove, finely chopped
2.5cm/1in piece fresh root ginger, peeled and grated
2.5ml/½ tsp cayenne pepper
675g/1½lb sweet potatoes
150ml/¼ pint/⅔ cup vegetable or chicken stock
225g/8oz spinach
45ml/3 tbsp pine nuts, toasted
salt and ground black pepper

1 Soak a clay potato pot in cold water for 20 minutes, then drain. Heat the oil in a large frying pan, add the onion, garlic, ginger and cayenne pepper and fry gently, stirring occasionally, for about 8 minutes, or until the onion is softened.

2 Peel the sweet potatoes and cut them into 2.5cm/1in chunks. Add the chunks to the frying pan and stir to coat them in the oil and spices.

COOK'S TIPS
• If you don't have a clay pot, use a deep baking dish – you won't need to soak it.
• To toast pine nuts, cook them for 3–4 minutes in a heavy pan, until they turn golden brown. Stir them occasionally and take care not to burn them.

VARIATIONS
• Add a drained, 400g/14oz can chickpeas to the potato mixture after 30 minutes cooking and stir well.
• Use baby new potatoes in place of the sweet potatoes.

3 Transfer the potato mixture to the clay pot and add the stock. Cover the pot and place in an unheated oven. Set the oven to 220°C/425°F/Gas 7 and cook for 50–60 minutes, or until the potatoes are just tender, stirring halfway through cooking.

4 Wash the spinach and shred roughly. Stir into the potatoes with the toasted pine nuts, re-cover the clay pot and cook for a further 5 minutes in the oven. Remove from the oven and leave to stand for 5 minutes. Adjust the seasoning and serve immediately.

ROASTED TOMATOES and GARLIC

These are so simple to prepare yet taste absolutely wonderful. Use a large, shallow earthenware dish that will allow the tomatoes to sear and char in a very hot oven.

SERVES 4

8 well-flavoured tomatoes (see Cook's Tip), halved
12 garlic cloves, unpeeled
60ml/4 tbsp extra virgin olive oil
3–4 bay leaves
salt and ground black pepper
45ml/3 tbsp fresh oregano leaves, to garnish

COOK'S TIP
If possible use ripe plum tomatoes for this recipe as they not only keep their shape and their delicious flavour, but also do not fall apart when roasted at such a high temperature. Leave the stalks on the tomatoes, if you like.

1 Preheat the oven to 230°C/450°F/Gas 8. Select a large, shallow ovenproof dish that will hold all the tomato halves snugly in a single layer. Arrange the tomatoes in the dish and tuck the whole, unpeeled garlic cloves evenly in among the tomatoes.

2 Brush the tomatoes with the oil, add the bay leaves and sprinkle black pepper over the top. Bake for about 45 minutes, or until the tomatoes have softened and are sizzling in the dish. Season with salt and more black pepper, if needed. Garnish with oregano leaves and serve.

SLOW-COOKED SPICED ONIONS

Onions marinated and baked in a spicy sauce are delicious with grilled or roasted meats. Choose a good, extra virgin olive oil for a rich flavour.

SERVES 4

675g/1½lb red or Spanish onions
90ml/6 tbsp olive or sunflower oil or a mixture of both
pinch of saffron threads
2.5ml/½ tsp ground ginger
5ml/1 tsp ground black pepper
5ml/1 tsp ground cinnamon
15ml/1 tbsp sugar

1 Slice the onions very thinly and place them in a shallow dish. Blend together the olive and/or sunflower oil, saffron, ground ginger, black pepper, cinnamon and sugar, and pour over the onions. Stir gently to mix, then set the onions aside for about 2 hours.

2 Preheat the oven to 160°C/325°F/Gas 3 and pour the onions and the marinade into a casserole or ovenproof dish.

COOK'S TIP
Onions grown in warmer climates are milder than those from cooler regions. Consequently Spanish onions have a mild, sweet flavour. Their skins are a rich golden colour and they are one of the largest varieties available.

3 Fold a large piece of foil into three and place over the top of the casserole or ovenproof dish, securing it with a lid.

4 Cook in the oven for 45 minutes, or until the onions are very soft, then increase the oven temperature to 200°C/400°F/Gas 6. Remove the lid and foil and cook for a further 5–10 minutes, or until the onions are lightly glazed. Serve immediately.

COOK'S TIP
When slicing onions, chop off the neck and just a little of the base to help the onion stay together. Score a line down the side of the onion and peel away the outer skin and first layer of flesh.

COURGETTES in TOMATO SAUCE

This rich-flavoured Mediterranean dish can be served hot or cold, either as a side dish or as part of a tapas meal. Cut the courgettes into fairly thick slices, so that they retain their texture and stay slightly crunchy.

SERVES 4

15ml/1 tbsp olive oil
1 onion, chopped
1 garlic clove, chopped
4 courgettes (zucchini), thickly sliced
400g/14oz can chopped tomatoes, drained
2 tomatoes, peeled, seeded and chopped
5ml/1 tsp vegetable bouillon powder
15ml/1 tbsp tomato purée (paste)
salt and ground black pepper

VARIATION
Add 1 or 2 sliced and seeded red, green or yellow (bell) peppers with the courgettes in step 1.

1 Heat the olive oil in a heavy pan, add the chopped onion and garlic and sauté for about 5 minutes, or until the onion is softened, stirring occasionally. Add the thickly sliced courgettes and cook for a further 5 minutes.

2 Add the canned and fresh tomatoes, bouillon powder and tomato purée. Stir well, then simmer for 10–15 minutes until the sauce is thickened and the courgettes are just tender. Season to taste and serve.

BAKED FENNEL with a CRUMB CRUST

The delicate aniseed flavour of baked fennel makes it a very good accompaniment to all kinds of dishes, from pasta and risotto to roast chicken.

SERVES 4

3 fennel bulbs, cut lengthwise into quarters
30ml/2 tbsp olive oil
1 garlic clove, chopped
50g/2oz/1 cup day-old wholemeal (whole-wheat) breadcrumbs
30ml/2 tbsp chopped fresh flat leaf parsley
salt and ground black pepper
a few fronds of fennel leaves, to garnish (optional)

COOK'S TIPS
• When buying fennel, look for compact, unblemished white-green bulbs. The leaves should look fresh and green. Tougher specimens will have bulbs that spread at the top.
• Fennel has a distinctive liquorice flavour, which particularly complements fish dishes. All parts of the plant are edible including the bulb, the celery-like stalks and the feathery leaves.

1 Cook the fennel in a pan of boiling salted water for 10 minutes. Preheat the oven to 190°C/375°F/Gas 5.

2 Drain the fennel and place in a large earthenware baking dish or baking tray, then brush with half of the olive oil.

VARIATION
To make a cheese-topped version, add 60ml/4 tbsp finely grated strong-flavoured cheese, such as mature (sharp) Cheddar, Red Leicester or Parmesan, to the breadcrumb mixture in step 3.

3 In a small bowl, mix together the chopped garlic, wholemeal breadcrumbs and chopped fresh flat leaf parsley, then stir in the rest of the olive oil. Sprinkle the mixture evenly over the fennel, then season well with salt and pepper.

4 Bake the fennel for about 30 minutes, or until it is tender and the breadcrumb topping is crisp and golden brown. Serve the baked fennel hot, garnished with a few fronds of fennel leaves, if you like.

CHEESE-TOPPED ROAST BABY VEGETABLES

A simple way of serving baby vegetables that really brings out their flavour.

SERVES 4

1kg/2¼lb mixed baby vegetables, such as aubergines (eggplant), onions or shallots, courgettes (zucchini), corn cobs and mushrooms
1 red (bell) pepper, seeded and cut into large pieces
1–2 garlic cloves, finely chopped
15–30ml/1–2 tbsp olive oil
30ml/2 tbsp chopped fresh mixed herbs
225g/8oz cherry tomatoes
115g/4oz/1 cup coarsely grated mozzarella cheese
salt and ground black pepper
black olives, to serve (optional)

1 Preheat the oven to 220°C/425°F/Gas 7. Cut the vegetables in half lengthwise.

2 Place the halved baby vegetables and pepper pieces in an ovenproof dish with the finely chopped garlic and plenty of salt and ground black pepper. Drizzle the oil over and toss the vegetables to coat them. Bake the vegetables for 20 minutes, or until they are tinged brown at the edges, stirring once during the cooking time.

3 Remove the ovenproof dish from the oven and stir in the chopped fresh mixed herbs. Sprinkle the cherry tomatoes over the surface and top with the coarsely grated mozzarella cheese. Return to the oven and bake for 5–10 minutes more until the cheese has melted and is bubbling. Serve immediately with black olives, if you like.

COOK'S TIP

This dish can also be made with a mixture of regular-sized vegetables. Simply chop them into bitesize pieces and continue from Step 2.

VARIATION

Use 2–3 sprigs of fresh rosemary in place of the chopped fresh mixed herbs.

BAKED SCALLOPED POTATOES with FETA CHEESE and OLIVES

Thinly sliced potatoes are cooked with Greek feta cheese and black and green olives and olive oil. This dish would also make a good light lunch served with a salad.

SERVES 4

- 4–6 large, unpeeled potatoes, total weight about 900g/2lb
- 150ml/¼ pint/⅔ cup extra virgin olive oil
- leaves from a sprig of rosemary
- 275g/10oz/2½ cups feta cheese, coarsely crumbled
- 115g/4oz/1 cup pitted mixed black and green olives
- 300ml/½ pint/1¼ cups hot vegetable stock
- salt and ground black pepper

1 Preheat the oven to 200°C/400°F/Gas 6. Bring a large pan of salted water to the boil and cook the potatoes, still in their skins, for 15 minutes until only just tender.

2 Drain the potatoes and set them aside until they are cool enough to handle. Carefully remove the peel from the potatoes using a small sharp knife and then cut them into thin slices.

3 Brush the base and sides of a 1.5 litre/2½ pint/6¼ cup rectangular ovenproof dish with some of the olive oil.

COOK'S TIP
Cooking the potatoes with their skins on not only helps to preserve their vitamin content, but will also ensure that the potatoes cook more evenly. If you prefer, peel them before they are cooked.

4 Arrange half the potatoes in the dish in an even layer. Top with half of the rosemary, cheese and olives and season with salt and pepper. Arrange the rest of the potatoes in an even layer on top.

5 Add the remaining rosemary leaves, crumbled cheese and olives, and drizzle with the remaining olive oil. Pour the hot vegetable stock over the top and season the top layer with salt and plenty of ground black pepper.

6 Bake for 35 minutes, covering the dish loosely with foil after about 20 minutes to prevent the potatoes from getting too brown. Serve hot, straight from the dish.

VARIATION
Thinly sliced sun-dried tomatoes would make a delicious addition.

POTATOES BAKED with FENNEL, ONIONS, GARLIC and SAFFRON

Potatoes, fennel and onions flavoured with garlic, saffron and spices make a sophisticated and attractive accompaniment to fish, chicken or egg-based main-course dishes.

SERVES 4–6

500g/1¼lb small waxy potatoes, cut into chunks or wedges
good pinch of saffron threads (12–15 threads)
1 head of garlic, separated into individual cloves
12 small red or yellow onions, peeled but left whole
3 fennel bulbs, cut into wedges, feathery tops reserved for garnish (optional)
4–6 fresh bay leaves
6–9 fresh thyme sprigs
175ml/6fl oz/¾ cup fish, chicken or vegetable stock
30ml/2 tbsp sherry or balsamic vinegar
2.5ml/½ tsp sugar
5ml/1 tsp fennel seeds, lightly crushed
2.5ml/½ tsp paprika
45ml/3 tbsp olive oil
salt and ground black pepper

1 Boil the potato chunks or wedges in a pan of boiling salted water for 8–10 minutes. Drain. Preheat the oven to 190°C/375°F/Gas 5. Soak the saffron threads in 30ml/2 tbsp warm water for 10 minutes.

2 Peel and finely chop two of the garlic cloves and set aside. Place the potato chunks or wedges, whole red or yellow onions, remaining unpeeled garlic cloves, fennel wedges, fresh bay leaves and fresh thyme sprigs in a large roasting pan or dish. Mix together the stock and the saffron and its soaking liquid in a jug (pitcher) or measuring cup.

3 Add the vinegar and sugar to the stock mixture, then pour the liquid over the vegetables. Stir in the fennel seeds, paprika, chopped garlic and oil, and season with salt and pepper.

4 Cook the vegetables in the oven for 1–1¼ hours, stirring occasionally, until they are just tender. Chop the reserved fennel tops, if using, and sprinkle them over the vegetables to garnish. Season the vegetables with more salt and pepper and serve immediately.

COOK'S TIP
Sherry vinegar has a rich, mellow flavour and it makes a good addition to a variety of sauces and dressings. It can be used simply to add extra piquancy to a dish. Try sprinkling a little over oven-roasted vegetables or add a teaspoon or two to soups, sauces or stews.

SAFFRON RICE with ONION and CARDAMOM

This delightfully fragrant, buttery pilaff is wonderful with both Indian and Middle-Eastern dishes, especially ones featuring fish, shellfish, chicken or lamb.

SERVES 4

350g/12oz/1¾ cups basmati rice
good pinch of saffron threads (about 15 threads)
25g/1oz/2 tbsp butter
1 onion, finely chopped
6 green cardamom pods, lightly crushed
5ml/1 tsp salt
2–3 fresh bay leaves
600ml/1 pint/2½ cups well-flavoured chicken or vegetable stock or water

1 Put the rice into a sieve and rinse well under cold running water. Tip it into a bowl, add cold water to cover and set aside to soak for 30–40 minutes. Drain in the sieve.

COOK'S TIP
After boiling, when all the liquid has been absorbed, basmati rice is set aside to finish cooking in its own heat and become tender. Wedging a folded dishtowel under the pan lid ensures the heat is not lost and the steam is absorbed.

2 Toast the saffron threads in a dry, heavy frying pan over a low heat for about 2 minutes, then place in a small bowl and add 30ml/2 tbsp warm water. Leave to soak for 10–15 minutes.

3 Melt the butter in the pan, then cook the onion with the cardamom pods very gently for 8–10 minutes, until soft and buttery yellow.

4 Add the drained rice to the pan and stir to coat the grains in the butter. Add the salt and bay leaves, then stir in the stock or water and saffron with its liquid. Bring the rice to the boil, stir, then reduce the heat to very low and cover tightly. Cook the rice for 10–12 minutes, until it has absorbed all the liquid.

5 Lay a clean, folded dishtowel over the pan under the lid and press on the lid to wedge it firmly in place. Leave the rice to stand for 10–15 minutes to continue cooking in its own heat.

6 Fluff up the grains of cooked rice with a fork. Place it in a warmed serving dish and serve immediately as an accompaniment to a spicy main course.

INDEX

apples: grouse with orchard fruit stuffing, 38
  noisettes of pork with creamy Calvados and apple sauce, 29
  pot-roast loin of pork with apple, 28
aubergines: Moroccan fish tagine, 61
  ratatouille, 72

baking dishes, 8–9
basmati rice and nut pilaff, 76
beans: Catalan potato and broad bean soup, 20
  Jamaican black bean pot, 74
  pancetta and broad bean risotto, 30
beef: fillet of beef Stroganoff, 36
  pot-roast beef with Guinness, 35
braising meat, 10
brill in red wine sauce, 57
broccoli, anchovy and pasta soup, 16
buckwheat noodles with cabbage, potatoes and cheese, 78

cabbage: buckwheat noodles with potatoes, cheese and, 78
carrots, braised with leeks, 84
casseroles, 10–11
  chicken casserole with winter vegetables, 42
  chicken with chickpeas and almonds, 46
  chicken with tomatoes and honey, 46
  coq au vin, 43
  fish with fregola, 59
  grouse with orchard fruit stuffing, 38
  Irish stew, 34
  Jamaican black bean pot, 74
  marinated pigeon in red wine, 39
  Mediterranean duck with harissa and saffron, 53
  ratatouille, 72
  Seville chicken, 45
  see also tagines
Catalan potato and broad bean soup, 20
cheese: baked scalloped potatoes with feta cheese and olives, 93
  buckwheat noodles with cabbage, potatoes and, 78
  cheese-topped roast baby vegetables, 92
  fettucine with butter and Parmesan, 78
  pasta shells with tomatoes and ricotta, 81
  pasta twists with pesto, 80
chicken: chicken and leek soup, 24
  chicken and prawn jambalaya, 50
  chicken baked with shallots, garlic and fennel, 44
  chicken biriani, 49
  chicken casserole with winter vegetables, 42
  chicken with chickpeas and almonds, 46
  chicken with tomatoes and honey, 46
  cooking techniques, 11
  coq au vin, 43
  risotto with chicken, 51
  Seville chicken, 45
chickpeas: chicken with almonds and, 46
chowder: clam, mushroom and potato, 23
clams: clam, mushroom and potato chowder, 23
  mussels and clams with lemon grass and coconut cream, 64
  seafood paella, 66
cod: cod and prawn green coconut curry, 62
  fish plaki, 60
  fish with fregola, 59

coq au vin, 43
courgettes in tomato sauce, 90
couscous: vegetable couscous with saffron and harissa, 77
curries: cod and prawn green coconut curry, 62
  spiced lamb with tomatoes and peppers, 31
  vegetable korma, 75

duck: Mediterranean duck with harissa and saffron, 53
  stir-fried crispy duck, 52

eggplant see aubergines
equipment, 8–9

fennel: baked fennel with a crumb crust, 90
  chicken baked with shallots, garlic and, 44
  potatoes baked with onions, garlic, saffron and, 94
fettucine with butter and Parmesan, 78
fish: fish plaki, 60
  fish stew with lemon grass, 63
  fish with fregola, 59
  Moroccan fish tagine, 61
  see also cod, tuna etc
free-standing cooking pots, 9
frittata: leek, red pepper and spinach, 70
  tuna frittata, 56

gammon: chicken and prawn jambalaya, 50
gingered seafood stir-fry, 65
grouse with orchard fruit stuffing, 38

Irish stew, 34
Italian farmhouse soup, 15

Jamaican black bean pot, 74
jambalaya, 50

lamb: Irish stew, 34
  Middle-Eastern roast lamb and potatoes, 33
  minted lamb stir-fry, 32
  Moroccan spiced lamb soup, 19
  spiced lamb with tomatoes and peppers, 31
leeks: baby leeks in red wine with aromatics, 85
  braised carrots with, 84
  braised leeks in tarragon cream, 84
  chicken and leek soup, 24
  frittata with red pepper, spinach and, 70
lentils: lentil and pasta soup, 14
  Mediterranean sausage and pesto soup, 18
lettuce: braised lettuce and peas with mint, 86

meat, cooking, 10–11
Mediterranean duck with harissa and saffron, 53
Mediterranean sausage and pesto soup, 18
Middle-Eastern roast lamb and potatoes, 33
Moroccan fish tagine, 61
Moroccan spiced lamb soup, 19
mushrooms: clam, mushroom and potato chowder, 23
  fillet of beef Stroganoff, 36
  venison sausages with red wine gravy, 37
mussels: mussels and clams with lemon grass and coconut cream, 64
  seafood paella, 66

noodles: buckwheat noodles with cabbage, potatoes and cheese, 78

okra and tomato tagine, 73
onions: potatoes baked with fennel, garlic, saffron and, 94
  saffron rice with cardamom and, 95
  slow-cooked spiced onions, 89

paella: seafood paella, 66
pan frying, 11
pancetta and broad bean risotto, 30
pasta: fish with fregola, 59
  pasta shells with tomatoes and ricotta, 81
  pasta squares and peas in broth, 16
  pasta twists with pesto, 80
pigeon: marinated pigeon in red wine, 39
pork: noisettes of pork with creamy Calvados and apple sauce, 29
  pot-roast loin of pork with apple, 28
pot-roasting, 10
pot-roasts: chicken with forty cloves of garlic, 48
  pot-roast beef with Guinness, 35
  pot-roast loin of pork with apple, 28
potatoes: baked scalloped, with feta cheese and olives, 93
  baked sea bream with tomatoes, 58
  buckwheat noodles with cabbage, cheese and, 78
  Catalan potato and broad bean soup, 20
  Irish stew, 34
  Middle-Eastern roast lamb and, 33
  new potatoes and vegetables baked Turkish-style, 71
  potatoes baked with fennel, onions, garlic and saffron, 94
  Spanish potato and garlic soup, 20
pots and pans, 8–9
prawns: chicken and prawn jambalaya, 50
  coconut and seafood soup, 25
  cod and prawn green coconut curry, 62
  seafood paella, 66

ratatouille, 72
red mullet: fish with fregola, 59
red snapper: fish with fregola, 59
rice: basmati rice and nut pilaff, 76
  chicken and prawn jambalaya, 50
  chicken biriani, 49
  saffron rice with onion and cardamom, 95
  seafood paella, 66
  Seville chicken, 45
risottos: pancetta and broad bean risotto, 30
  risotto with chicken, 51
  seafood risotto, 67
roasts: Middle-Eastern roast lamb and potatoes, 33
  see also pot-roasts

saffron rice with onion and cardamom, 95
sausages: Mediterranean sausage and pesto soup, 18
  venison sausages with red wine gravy, 37
sea bream with tomatoes, 58
seafood: gingered seafood stir-fry, 65
  seafood paella, 66
  seafood risotto, 67
Seville chicken, 45
shallots, chicken baked with garlic, fennel and, 44
shrimp see prawns

soups: broccoli, anchovy and pasta soup, 16
  Catalan potato and broad bean soup, 20
  chicken and leek soup, 24
  clam, mushroom and potato chowder, 23
  coconut and seafood soup, 25
  corn and potato chowder, 22
  Italian farmhouse soup, 15
  lentil and pasta soup, 14
  Mediterranean sausage and pesto soup, 18
  Moroccan spiced lamb soup, 19
  pasta squares and peas in broth, 16
  Spanish potato and garlic soup, 20
Spanish potato and garlic soup, 20
spinach: frittata with leek, red pepper and, 70
  spinach braised with sweet potatoes, 87
stews see casseroles
stir-fries: gingered seafood stir-fry, 65
  minted lamb stir-fry, 32
  stir-fried crispy duck, 52
stir-frying, 11
sweet potatoes: spinach braised with, 87

tagines: Moroccan fish, 61
  okra and tomato, 73
techniques, 10–11
tomatoes: baked sea bream with, 58
  chicken and prawn jambalaya, 50
  chicken with honey and, 46
  courgettes in tomato sauce, 90
  okra and tomato tagine, 73
  pasta shells with tomatoes and ricotta, 81
  peeling, 10–11
  ratatouille, 72
  roasted tomatoes and garlic, 88
  spiced lamb with peppers and, 31
tuna frittata, 56

vegetables: cheese-topped roast baby vegetables, 92
  chicken casserole with winter vegetables, 42
  Italian farmhouse soup, 15
  new potatoes and vegetables baked Turkish-style, 71
  ratatouille, 72
  vegetable couscous with saffron and harissa, 77
  vegetable korma, 75
venison sausages with red wine gravy, 37

water chestnuts: stir-fried crispy duck, 52
wine: braised baby leeks in red wine, 85
  coq au vin, 43
  marinated pigeon in red wine, 39
  venison sausages with red wine gravy, 37
woks, 8